BELIEF

BUILDING UNSHAKEABLE CONFIDENCE

THE WIN FROM WITHIN SERIES

DR JO LUKINS

Names, characters and places have been adapted to share the concepts while protecting the confidentiality of individuals.

ISBN: 978-1-7635127-0-2 (Paperback)

ISBN: 978-1-7635127-1-9 (eBook)

Editor: Marinda Wilkinson

Elite Edge Publishing

www.drjolukins.com

To the athletes, coaches, and teams that have trusted me to work with them on their sporting journey, hamamas.

CONTENTS

From the Author xi
Introduction xvii

1. PRIME YOUR MIND: ACTIVATING YOUR INNER COACH 1
The inner coach 3
Every expert was once a beginner 7
The mantra advantage 9
Once upon a time 11

2. THE HEART OF PERFORMANCE 13
Defining your values 16
What are your values? 19
Setting individual values 22
Understand your values before setting goals 25

3. SHARPENED CURIOSITY 33
Entering the TARDIS 34
Timeless tools for navigating thoughts 36
Reflecting on past experiences 38
Thinking in the present 39
Thinking in the future 40
The power of wonder 43
Courage rising: Embracing vulnerability 46
The knowledge + curiosity loop: Increasing your curiosity mindset 49
Adopting the mindset of the curious observer 52

4. FROM FIXED MINDSET TO FLEXIBLE EXCELLENCE 57
Fortunately/unfortunately 59
Perfect is the enemy of excellence 62
Switching your mindset 64
Key takeaways and inner coach guidance: 67

5. CONQUER DOUBT AND NEGATIVITY 71
Don't think about the Eiffel Tower 71
Mind races: Taming mental overdrive 75
Seven traps of excessive mental investment 77
So, if not overthinking, what is it? 80
How, then, can we define this for ourselves in a better way? 81
Believe it to achieve it: The power of self-efficacy 84
Why imposter syndrome doesn't exist 87

6. NAVIGATING THE ROLLER COASTER OF EXPECTATIONS 91
Mastering emotional terrain: Navigate and dominate 94
Utilizing the inner coach: Mental success through non-selection 97
Turning errors into opportunities: using reflection, sharing and learning 100

7. STRATEGIES FOR MENTAL OBSTACLES 105
Winning against the negativity odds: How you can flip the score 106
Defusion from our thoughts 110

8. TRIUMPH OVER TRIALS 115
Hope ignites: The foundation of optimism 115
The inescapable truth about ignoring thoughts: Why you can't just "block it out" 118
Match point emotions: Decoding the thin line between tennis nerves and excitement 121
Belief in action: How cue words can set you up for success 124
The rapid disposal method: Eliminating unhelpful thoughts 126

9. EMOTIONAL RESILIENCE FOR PEAK PERFORMANCE 131
Embracing sorrow: The unexpected power of sadness 132
From disgust to discovery 133
Fearless leaps: Mastering anxiety in athletics 135

Raging storms and calm seas: The highs and lows of anger 138
Unlocking moments: Finding joy in every challenge 141
A word of caution 144

10. MIND'S EYE MASTERY 147
How does mental rehearsal work? 148
How does mental rehearsal assist athletic performance? 149
WYSIWYG 152
Visual victory: Better performance through visualization 154
In a nutshell 159

11. RISE STRONGER IN TIMES OF INJURY 163
Defying doubt: Triumphing through optimism 165
Rebounding stronger: Navigating injury setbacks with resilience 168
Returning from injury 173

12. COMPETE WITH BELIEF: THE NEXT LEVEL AWAITS 177
The inner coach and you 177
Journaling 2.0 178
Prime your mind: Activating your inner coach 180
Beliefs and values: The heart of performance 181
Sharpened curiosity: Mastering focus in the right moment 182
From fixed mindset to flexible excellence: Shifting limits to triumphs 183
Conquer doubt and negativity: Unlock your competitive edge 184
Belief vs. disappointment: Navigating the roller coaster of expectations 185
Conquer mental obstacles: Strategies for overcoming negative bias 186
Triumph over trials: Harnessing helpful thinking for victory 187
Mood mastery: Using emotional resilience for peak performance 188
Mind's eye mastery: Crafting your winning playbook 189

Rise stronger: Strengthening the mind for injury and recovery 190
What's next? From *Belief* to *Compete* 191

Appendix: Creating customized values for your team 193
About Dr. Jo 201
A Note from Dr. Jo 203
Stay connected: With Dr. Jo 205
Read more with Dr. Jo 207
Bonus offer: The Good Sleep Guide 209
Facebook group 211

Belief is the unwavering conviction that what you aspire to, you can indeed attain.

With belief, aspirations transform into reality.

FROM THE AUTHOR

Welcome to *Belief*, a collection of wisdom crafted for athletes seeking the winning formula.

As we know, success in sports isn't a leisurely walk in the park; it's an unpredictable journey resembling a roller-coaster ride. Expect obstacles and setbacks that will push your limits. Athletes often set clear goals, yet the path ahead is full of surprises. Finding the right strategies can feel like a race against time when unexpected hurdles arise. In these pages, I've carefully outlined the realities of success. Some sections will captivate you, others will require dedication, and a few might seem daunting but hold the key to progress. So, prepare for the ups and downs, and let's navigate this journey together, unlocking your well-deserved success.

The understanding of high performance in sports has evolved significantly. Gone are the days of the old-school "suck it up" mentality; today, there's a more informed perspective on what it takes for athletes to excel. Graduating from university in the early 1990s, I found myself in some rather entertaining conversations about my new profession. The public's perception of psychology varied widely, from believing that I could read minds to possessing the superpower of controlling people's behaviors (if only that were the case!). Furthermore, psychology was often narrowly viewed as a discipline primarily concerned with individuals on a troubled path, dedicated to helping them overcome mental and emotional distress and little else. It was commonly associated with conditions such as anxiety, depression, borderline personality disorder, and similar challenges. This perception was rooted in the discipline's historical focus, spanning a couple of centuries, as a profession devoted to addressing the complexities of the human experience and offering remedies for such difficulties.

However, as the late 1980s approached, the profession underwent a significant transformation. Thanks to the curiosity of forward-thinking individuals, the long-standing focus on dysfunction and distress that had persisted for centuries was about to take a different turn. Professor Donald Clift posed a game-changing question: "What if we studied what's right with people?" The focus within the profession started to turn to the science of success, performance, flourishing, and achievement.

Simultaneously, others were asking similar optimistic and curious questions, including Professor Martin Seligman, a prominent figure in psychology since the 1970s. His early research delved into learned helplessness, a study initially conducted with dogs who were exposed to repetitive negative stimuli. The results were eye-opening. Most of the dogs gave up when things didn't go their way repeatedly. They assumed change was futile and a positive outcome was unattainable. However, this wasn't the case for all of them. This realization of attitudes impacting outcomes led to a shift in focus, steering Seligman's research toward the concept of learned optimism.

Learned optimism recognizes that some individuals possess the resilience to pick themselves up and persevere, regardless of life's challenges. This finding profoundly impacted our understanding of how people cope with repeated adversity. Seligman's notable contributions led to his election as President of the American Psychological Association. This prestigious role elevated his standing within the profession and allowed him to focus his research on a subject of his choice, generously supported by significant funding.

For his presidential term, Seligman chose to steer the profession toward focusing on positive psychology, which, in its simplest form, revolves around the science of what goes well in human life. Since then, psychology has embraced a more deliberate exploration of positive psychology in research and practical applications. It became more organized and structured, with dedicated journals and a growing body of evidence-based knowledge.

So, what did all this mean for sports psychology? The broader questions the profession was now asking about happiness, success, achievement, and well-being in human experience naturally aligned with the concerns of sports psychology. Importantly, it enabled sports psychology to focus its research efforts more effectively on understanding success, achievement, and fulfillment in sports. It provided a deeper insight into the human psyche when athletes and teams stand on the brink of success.

Seligman's work with Olympic swimmers, notably the champion Matt Biondi, played a pivotal role in raising profound questions about high-performance psychology. The ripple effect of his research significantly enhanced our understanding of high performance. This shift in the discipline opened the door to my first research project, which explored the relationship between children's self-esteem and how they experience disappointment and success in sports. Several years later, my PhD research delved into the influence of belief, optimism, and pessimism on the risk of injury and athletes' recovery from those injuries. This study will be a focal point when we examine the role of belief in injury prevention and rehabilitation.

Moving on from the history lesson, let's return to my early '90s journey in sporting clubs. It's safe to say that there was some understandable confusion about what I could do initially. As a recent graduate, I wasn't entirely sure myself! Perhaps you can recall when you ventured into a new field—enthusiastic but inexperienced. I didn't have the precise terminology back then, but, indeed, every expert was once a beginner, and we all need a place to start and someone willing to give us a chance.

In my quest to find a niche for my interest in sports psychology in the regional areas of northern Australia, I did what I would advise any recent graduate to do—say "yes." If there's an opportunity and a willingness to try something, take it on, even if it feels like biting off more than you can chew. I stretched well beyond my comfort zone during my first four years of work. I became a university tutor (tutoring was manageable, but tackling the teaching of second-year statistics did raise my blood pressure!); I worked as a telephone counselor; I collaborated with an employee assistance agency, which involved flying to mining sites after critical incidents; and whenever someone invited me to speak at an event (often for free), I eagerly seized the opportunity, recognizing that I was honing my presentation skills and making my name known. It was perhaps a combination of bravery and naivety, but I took the plunge. This daring approach eventually led me to a pivotal decision in 1996 that would shape my career trajectory.

Rugby League holds a dominant position in Australian sports. Among the various football codes—Australian Football League, Rugby Union, and Football/Soccer—Rugby League reigns supreme in my region. In 1995, North Queensland experienced a historic moment by introducing a team, the North Queensland Cowboys, into the Australian National Rugby League competition. In their inaugural year, the team operated without a sports psychologist, and the club had minimal staff in its early stages. Key stakeholders wore multiple hats, juggling numerous roles to get the team on the field. Players were semi-professional, and many helped build the stadium and coaching facilities during their work hours as tradespeople before changing into footy shorts for training.

In 1996, a new coach, the New Zealand legend Sir Graham Lowe, arrived at the club. I don't recall precisely how I secured an interview with him or found my way into his office. Still, I remember the setting—an unassuming demountable building in the middle of what would become the members' car park. Graham generously offered his time and shared his aspirations for the team from a mental perspective. He expressed the need for someone on his staff to introduce the team to sports psychology concepts, explain how it could be applied in Rugby League, and then work directly with the players to enhance their mental game. To this day, I vividly remember him leaning back in his chair at the end of our conversation, holding direct eye contact, and posing the question, "Essentially, Jo, I'm looking for a combination between Sigmund Freud and Lois Lane. Are you up for it?" I held his gaze and replied with unwavering confidence, "Absolutely." More than 25 years later, I admit I had no clear idea of what he asked of me. However, I am reasonably sure that I was one of the first, if not the first, sports psychologists he had employed, giving me the unique opportunity to define the role.

Decades have passed, and I've spent thousands of hours working with athletes, coaches, and teams. Thankfully, I now have a much clearer understanding of what sports psychology entails and how it can be integrated into an athlete's life. By paying attention to the mental aspect of your sporting journey, you will equip yourself with the tools to conquer challenges and achieve the success you deserve.

Sport allows you to test your physical, tactical, and mental skills—all three are essential for success. *Belief* is here to help you comprehend and master your mental game. This book will guide you on a journey to explore the different elements of your psychological game, helping you become a winner, both in and out of competition. I look forward to sharing this journey with you.

Shine bright, Dr. Jo

INTRODUCTION

In sports psychology, understanding how athletes behave can get entangled in complex jargon, making simple things sound overly complicated. Terms like "grit" or "mental toughness" might be tossed around without clear explanations. This book seeks to untangle the confusion, explaining concepts clearly with relatable examples. The goal is to keep things straightforward so you don't get bogged down in technicalities but gain insights that directly impact your performance on the field, court, pool, track, or arena.

Exploring the workings of our minds in psychology is like stepping into another land. It takes everyday ideas and dissects them in various ways, adding layers and challenges. Its aim is always to understand human behavior better and examine it through the scrutiny of science. In the context of this book, by combining your sporting wisdom, with the ideas and strategies presented, you can elevate your confidence and belief to new levels.

In psychological theories, even the most straightforward concepts undergo examination by different experts, offering diverse perspectives. It's intelligent, but the abundance of viewpoints can become overwhelming. This book steps in as a guide, connecting the complex world of psychology with real-life situations athletes encounter. It breaks down intricate ideas without oversimplifying, providing a shortcut to understanding the concepts without mental overload.

In writing this book, I've pulled together some of the tools and lessons I've shared with the many athletes I've worked with across a diverse range of sports. Within this book, you will learn the critical lessons to develop an unshakeable belief to take to your next performance. It offers you a steadfast companion on your journey to achieve more outstanding athletic excellence, working hand in hand with you as you learn these valuable lessons and put them into practice.

In *Belief*, we will address these essential questions:

- How does belief develop?
- How does belief become a habit of thinking?
- Why does belief come effortlessly to some and remain out of reach for others?
- How can belief be strengthened?
- How can we hold on to our belief?

A tip on how to get the most from this book

If you're anything like me, your bookshelf is a treasure trove of timeless non-fiction reads. Many of these books become like old friends, companions I revisit and reread at various times. I hope that *Belief* is a book that will be more than a read for you. Please use the opportunity to put into action some of its strategies and use them to build your belief.

One way to gain further benefit beyond the pages, is to engage in the practice of *journaling*. Journaling is a strategy that has yielded incredible results for many of the athletes I've worked with, athletes like you, who understand the value of pushing boundaries and unlocking their potential. Beyond being a mere record of your thoughts, journaling serves as a powerful tool. Whether it's aiding in a restful slumber, providing a safe outlet for intense emotions, or acting as a platform for innovative problem-solving, journaling has proven its worth.

But how do I journal? When I try to open the book, a blank page stares back at me . . .

When journaling is a new pursuit, it can feel awkward and make you feel self-conscious, perhaps even embarrassed. That discomfort is a good sign that you are stretching your boundaries. So, what do you write? Well, whatever you want! As a start, I suggest that you organize your thinking, reflect on your progress, and plan moving forward.

What if I don't like writing? That's okay; there is a way for everyone to journal. I have had athletes who substituted the diary for the voice memo app on their phones, dictating their thoughts to keep a record. I've also had some who use other apps to transcribe what is said, so you still end up with a written version! The key purpose of journaling is to reflect and capture a moment in time. It is fine to use any method you find most comfortable.

If it helps to get you started, the following are common reflective questions I consider when journaling:

Learning – What did I learn during the session (about the activity and myself)?
Application – How can I apply these lessons moving forward?
Curiosity – What remains unknown? What further questions do I have?

For ongoing inspiration, you can follow the journal prompts I put in my Facebook group (Winning Strategies) every Tuesday: click here.

So, as you delve into *Belief*, consider incorporating journaling as a parallel exercise. Let these pages inspire your thoughts and ignite your desire to document your journey and self-discoveries. Just as the athletes I've worked with, have found tremendous value in this practice, you too, can uncover a world of insight and advancement. You have room at the conclusion of every chapter to jot down extra notes regarding the content.

This book, along with *Compete*, the second book in this series, combine to build confidence and capability, regardless of the challenge.

Belief, the development of unwavering confidence, is within reach as you forge ahead with determination and the best mindset on the path to success in competitive sports.

Belief is your how-to guide for championship thinking.

Time to begin!

CHAPTER ONE
PRIME YOUR MIND: ACTIVATING YOUR INNER COACH

"The mind is the limit. As long as the mind can envision the fact that you can do something, you can do it, as long as you really believe 100 percent."
Arnold Schwarzenegger

JACK OCCUPIED the chair across from me in my office, his broad frame appearing somewhat ill at ease in the seat. His fingers rhythmically tapped on the table, revealing the nervous energy he brought with him. Jack and I had a history of roughly 18 months; he was a hockey team member for a team I had worked with for several years. However, this marked his inaugural visit to my office. As I invited him to share the reason that prompted our meeting, he seemed uncertain about where to begin, suppressing the urge to let his words spill forth.

"I've always been the big kid," he began. "The one who was physically larger than others my age, and it made me successful from an early age. Fortunately, my old man taught me the value of hard work, so I remained competitive even when the other kids caught up to me in size. I was good at what I did and knew the habits that kept me in the game. But recently, I've been struggling with a feeling that's hard to describe. I should be more confident than I am. The coaches and my manager insist I can go all the way if I don't sabotage myself. Sometimes, doubt creeps in from nowhere. It doesn't make sense, yet it makes me second-guess myself, leading to overthinking and mistakes. I need to find a way to boost my confidence and have the self-belief everyone tells me I should have."

While Jack's circumstances were unique, his challenge was far from uncommon. I had heard similar concerns more times than I could count. Athletes who seemingly had it all, with outstanding fitness and skills, impressive sports intelligence, an exemplary work ethic, or a genetic advantage, making the challenge appear effortless. Yet, despite all these assets, a single formidable obstacle stood in the way: self-doubt, nagging thoughts, personal uncertainties, and hesitation in making decisions. It was a lowered sense of self-belief that left them on shaky ground.

A lack of belief can sow seeds of uncertainty and anxiety and wreak havoc on an athlete's confidence. It is common in high performance, and often leads to feeling overwhelmed. It certainly can feel like you are the only person it's happening to, partly because its very nature means that you won't admit it or talk to others about it. The silver lining for Jack was that his belief could be strengthened. During that initial session, Jack and I began crafting a plan to help him cultivate the unwavering confidence he needed. I explained that understanding belief involved specific steps and strategies supported by psychological science, which could guide him toward the success he deserved. The key was knowing how to unlock that potential.

Consider this: belief is not a fixed state, but a mindset you can actively mold. Self-doubt doesn't have to seal your fate with underperformance. Instead, think of belief as your guiding light on your sporting journey. It's a beacon of hope, a light that can lead you to unexpected success and triumph.

THE INNER COACH

The symphony of sounds in an athlete's world—the crowd's thunderous applause, the guidance from a coach, and the camaraderie among teammates—all play integral roles in shaping their experience. However, arguably, an athlete's most pivotal dialogue isn't with their coach, fans, or teammates. It's the conversations they have with themselves.

Whether part of a team or competing individually, every athlete engages in an internal dialogue, a constant stream of thoughts that profoundly influences their performance. This inner conversation, often referred to as self-talk, possesses the unique power to bolster confidence, enhance focus, and nurture resilience. The "personal pep talks" summon courage in the face of formidable opposition or encourage perseverance during grueling training sessions. It's the kind, reassuring voice that whispers, "You've done enough," or the dominant voice that barks, "You must do more!"

For each athlete, this habitual self-talk becomes their inner coach, guiding their strategy, pushing them past perceived limits, and maintaining their motivation when faced with adversity. It might be a tennis player calmly reminding themselves to stay composed and focused before a crucial serve or a marathon runner softly repeating, "Next step," to ward off fatigue.

On the flip side, the inner coach can sometimes morph into a voice of negativity, uttering phrases like, "You can't do it," "You're destined to fail," or "You're hopeless." Each message carries significant weight, propelling the athlete down a path that aligns with their belief and creates the outcome they wish to avoid.

Let's consider how the inner coach might play a part in the outcome for a squad of high-performing swimmers, all sharing physical strength, technical prowess, dedicated coaching, and unwavering commitment. What distinguishes those who will perform well from those who will reach the pinnacle of their competition? Countless research studies underscore the pivotal role that an athlete's self-talk, reflecting their belief, plays in their performance. The swimmer who stands poised on the starting blocks, both physically and mentally prepared, with a clear understanding of their race plan, is poised to deliver their best performance. In contrast, the equally well-prepared swimmer who repeatedly tells themselves that the competition is too good and they aren't ready, takes to the blocks shaking and feeling physically ill. Success is formed upon habits, the repeated small actions that create the foundation of achievement. Just as we cultivate behavioral habits, we also develop thinking habits. These are the consistent patterns of thought that we repeatedly engage in, shaping the course of our journey. It's a realization for both swimmers that echoes the wisdom of Henry Ford's quote:

"Whether you think you can or think you can't, you're right."

To illustrate this point, let's delve into a pivotal research study that included one of the world's most accomplished swimmers as a participant. Dr. Martin Seligman, recognized as a pioneer in positive psychology (the science of what goes well), conducted an experiment that shed light on the influence of belief. His findings, published in *Psychological Science* journal in 1990, provide a fascinating insight into how an athlete's mindset can profoundly impact their performance.

In the world of Olympic swimming competitions, Matt Biondi's journey to greatness offers a compelling illustration of how positive psychology and belief can play a pivotal role in achieving remarkable athletic feats. Seligman's research allowed him to anticipate Biondi's ability to bounce back even after experiencing disappointment in his first two races at the 1988 Seoul Olympics.

In this study, Seligman administered the Attributional Style Questionnaire (ASQ) to a group of highly trained swimmers from the University of California Berkeley swim team. The ASQ is a tool that assesses how individuals react to various situations and can distinguish between those with an optimistic and pessimistic outlook on the world. Importantly, this tool revealed the critical role that one's belief system plays in their performance. After completing the test, each swimmer was tasked with delivering their best performance in the pool for their preferred distance.

The fascinating twist in the experiment followed when researchers informed each swimmer that their reported times were worse than their actual performance, setting the stage for perceived disappointment. Subsequently, following the news of the disappointing time, the athletes were given another chance to swim their best race after a brief rest period.

The results were enlightening. Disheartened by their perceived failure, swimmers with lower beliefs found it mentally challenging to recover from the setback, leading to even worse times in their subsequent swim. In stark contrast, those with a stronger belief, driven by determination and optimism, performed better in their second effort.

The results suggested that individuals with a stronger belief (when faced with adverse outcomes) maintained a positive outlook, invested additional effort, and improved their performance on the second attempt. Those with lowered beliefs were less likely to exert extra effort, and more likely to maintain a more pessimistic outlook, and underperform.

This leads us to the remarkable journey of American swimmer Matt Biondi. In the 1988 Seoul Olympics, Biondi was a firm favorite for multiple medals. Instead, he commenced the meet underperforming with the disappointment of finishing third in the 200-meter freestyle and narrowly losing the 100-meter butterfly in the final two meters to Anthony Nesty of Suriname. Commentators were quick to speculate that such defeats might be impossible for any athlete to come back from. However, Martin Seligman knew better. He recognized that Matt Biondi had been one of the Berkeley swimmers in his study and had tested in the top quarter for belief. Despite the initial setbacks, Biondi went on to win an astonishing five gold medals in Seoul.

In the pool and life beyond, perseverance and optimism are key factors of success. A strong belief equips individuals to rebound swiftly from failure, propelling them to higher performance levels. While belief is often considered an inherent trait, research demonstrates that it can be enhanced, leading to significant changes in confidence and performance.

Having Jack in my office, much like countless others before him, instilled confidence in my ability to help. I recognized that belief wasn't an inherent or fixed trait—it was a mental strength that could be cultivated. With the appropriate guidance, resources, and encouragement, anyone could build the groundwork for robust mental belief and pave the way for future success. Jack needed to recognize his inner coach and develop the skills to guide himself in an informed and evidence-based way.

Much like the studies conducted by Seligman and other researchers have shown, the potential for improving athletic performance through belief evaluation and psychological training is evident. Athletes, armed with the right tools, can actively nurture, and strengthen their beliefs, thereby paving the way to a brighter future and greater success.

In team sports, while coordination and communication with teammates are crucial, an athlete's internal dialogue plays a pivotal role. Whether it's a soccer player reminding themselves to stay patient while seeking a scoring opportunity or a basketball player mentally rehearsing a free throw while encouraging themselves, the ability to manage and harness this inner conversation significantly impacts an athlete's performance. The inner coach can become a formidable opponent, filling the athlete's mind with doubt and fear when it's negative, or it can be their greatest ally when it provides honest and helpful guidance, fostering a mindset of confidence, resilience, and unwavering determination.

Working with this inner coach, transforming it into a voice of positive reinforcement and strategic advice, is just as important as the physical conditioning demands of sport. Mastering the art of self-talk empowers athletes to reach new heights in their performance and turn their most significant critics—themselves—into their most supportive fans. An athlete's most crucial conversation is the one they have with themselves; it's a dialogue that holds the power to shape their athletic destiny.

Throughout this book, we will delve into this inner dialogue. Your ability to trust in yourself is the ultimate conversation in creating success. It doesn't mean you won't encounter challenges along the way; the road to victory is never smooth. However, belief provides the mental guidance to trust yourself within your sport and get the job done.

As your belief develops, you will learn strategies to bounce forward from disappointment (resilience), a clear understanding of what helps you perform well (systems), a mindset that wonders and continues to ask questions (curiosity), and a recognition of what you have achieved (accomplishments), giving you unshakeable confidence in your ability to move forward.

EVERY EXPERT WAS ONCE A BEGINNER

When we watch experts at their craft—Tom Brady making a touchdown, Serena Williams securing a grand slam, or Cristiano Ronaldo hitting the back of the net from almost any range, it is hard to imagine them as a beginner, at the time in their lives when they did not possess that skill. But watch any young child pick up the basketball for the first time or draw their leg back to kick a soccer ball, and you will witness a beginner in action. When we watch children learning sports, we don't expect them to get it right the first time. We encourage them through their misses and errors and understand they are a necessary part of the journey. In short, we acknowledge that the beginning is the start of the path to mastery. Starting is often tricky, but watch the joy and determination young children bring to the beginning phase of learning. They don't expect competency from the outset. They can watch someone else with the skill, and instead of comparing and declaring defeat, they are inspired to keep trying. They start again and continue practicing until competency results.

What are your memories of learning something new as a child? For me, it was learning to ride a bike. All the children in my street owned bicycles and used to fly down the hill together, off for an adventure, and I longed to join them. Then, one birthday, the greatest gift ever: a new bike. From memory, it was bright yellow, with tassels flowing from the handlebars. I couldn't wait to get out in the street and ride with my friends. I remember being slightly annoyed that training wheels in my yard supported my first journey, but I was determined the need for this aid would be short-lived. I rode around for some time until my father decided I was ready for the next phase in my learning and removed one of the training wheels. I'm not sure how much this helped my progression. Not yet having the proprioceptive cues to hold my balance, I shifted all my weight to the side of the bike with the training wheel and continued to ride with relative ease. That transition was short-lived, and soon, I was to find myself *sans* training wheels and at the helm of a two-wheel bicycle. What ensued over the following days was a lesson in the difficulties of balance and the harsh reality of grazed knees and elbows while I gradually improved. Like most children, perseverance prevailed, and it wasn't long before the cues of balance kicked in, and I was soon flying down the streets with my neighbors. Now, decades after that painful lesson in learning, I can return to a bike, and my balance returns almost instantly. Every expert was once a beginner.

I've shared with you one of my many stories of being a beginner, and I know you have countless stories of your own: when you learned to write, was taught to swim, perhaps the first time you learned to cook for yourself. We all start with low abilities and matching expectations, but we build expertise through trial and (plenty of) error. Expect that this may happen to you while reading *Belief*. I will share ideas, strategies, and techniques, and I envisage many will be new for you. Some concepts will come quickly for you, and the change process will be smooth. You may need to put your mental "training wheels" on for others. The good news is I will be with you for the journey, to help pick you up, until you are ready to ride by yourself.

Most people I've encountered prefer their lives to be under control and predictable. These states bring a sense of calm, minimizing disruption in our daily routines. Change, by default, tends to feel like the opposite of this stability. Transitioning from our current state to a new version of ourselves, whatever that change entails, demands a fresh approach, a degree of disruption, and an acceptance that learning the ropes of this new reality can be messy.

This book introduces novel strategies, behaviors, and ways of thinking designed to propel you closer to your goals and achievements. I won't sugarcoat it: It won't be a walk in the park. If it were that easy, everyone would be doing it. However, I can assure you that the journey will be worthwhile.

THE MANTRA ADVANTAGE

Embarking on change, even in small increments, demands a willing mindset. My approach to effective change involves acknowledging that initially, it often feels challenging and may get messy in the middle. The real rewards and discoveries come once the change is established. Acceptance forms the core of your success throughout this transformative journey. The key to cultivating a change mindset, embracing the process, and welcoming it as the way forward lies in the ability to use acceptance to reconcile the highs and lows.

Acceptance means understanding that discomfort and minor setbacks are part of the journey. Feeling frustrated when things get uncomfortable is normal. Just because you haven't reached your goal yet doesn't mean you're off course–you're likely precisely where you need to be! I have a mantra for times of change, a word or phrase to encourage navigating through challenging times. We'll delve deeper into mantras later in the book, but let's focus on this one for now.

Imagine I'm incorporating a new mobility program into my week as an "extra" activity after my regular gym sessions. Initially, it sounds like a great plan, but reality hits when the gym session ends, and the prospect of an additional 20 minutes to complete the program doesn't feel appealing. My feet are itching to head out the door, my hand reaching for my keys to go home. My mantra kicks in these moments: "It's kind of the point." This mantra reminds me during discomfort that I am navigating a period of change, a journey toward improvement and something better. It acknowledges that change can be slow and frustrating, but if I'm on the path to something new, I'm precisely where I need to be.

For those tempted to critique my mantra's grammatical precision, it might not pass an English major's scrutiny. Still, it's how I say it in my head, making it practical for me!

You might prefer another phrase to guide you through the frustrations of change. I share this from the outset because as you explore various skills and strategies in this book, you'll encounter times when starting initially feels great, but the journey may pull you back into old habits, causing discomfort. Hang in there. Remember that progress takes time; setbacks are signs you're moving closer to success. If you have a phrase that fuels your perseverance, now is a good time to jot it down and keep it close:

____

Belief is not intended as a motivational book. I'll be pleased if you read, absorb, and feel motivated, but motivation is a fleeting moment. Something that can sit within us for several minutes or hours. But motivation only lasts briefly; it's like showering, so you must do it daily. Belief, however, is more enduring. When we form a foundation of belief, it sets us up to reach our potential. When we've scaffolded our mindset to be strong in its belief, we can ride through the challenges of high-performance moments, first times, high pressures, worry, and disappointments, and be ready to reset and go again.

ONCE UPON A TIME

Humans learn through stories. At our heart, we are curious souls, so understanding our own lives through the stories of others is a helpful way to learn. When you hear someone else's story, you can consider how that fits with your own life, what the similarities and differences are, what of their story makes sense to you, and what is inconsistent. Each consideration is an opportunity to grow. For this reason, I like to include stories within my writing. Within *Belief*, I will weave the stories of those who have gone before you for you to understand, consider, and use as a reference point for your learning. All the stories I will share are true. However, please know that key identifying factors (age, sport, gender, or name) have been changed to preserve the anonymity of the personas.

Building belief can feel like a tenuous journey. By recognizing that confidence needs to build, self-talk can improve, and a self-assured demeanor is sought, belief can fluctuate. Perhaps you have realized that your mindset needs to change, but you are unsure how to do that. Your intentions are great, but you don't clearly understand how to make the changes. It can feel frustrating to see the confidence of others and not know how to attain it. By building an unshakeable belief, you will have a clear path of thinking to get you closer to success. While having belief won't safeguard you from disappointments along the way, it will ensure you can navigate the knockbacks more resiliently and robustly.

Building a belief and a performance mindset takes time—it will be worth it.

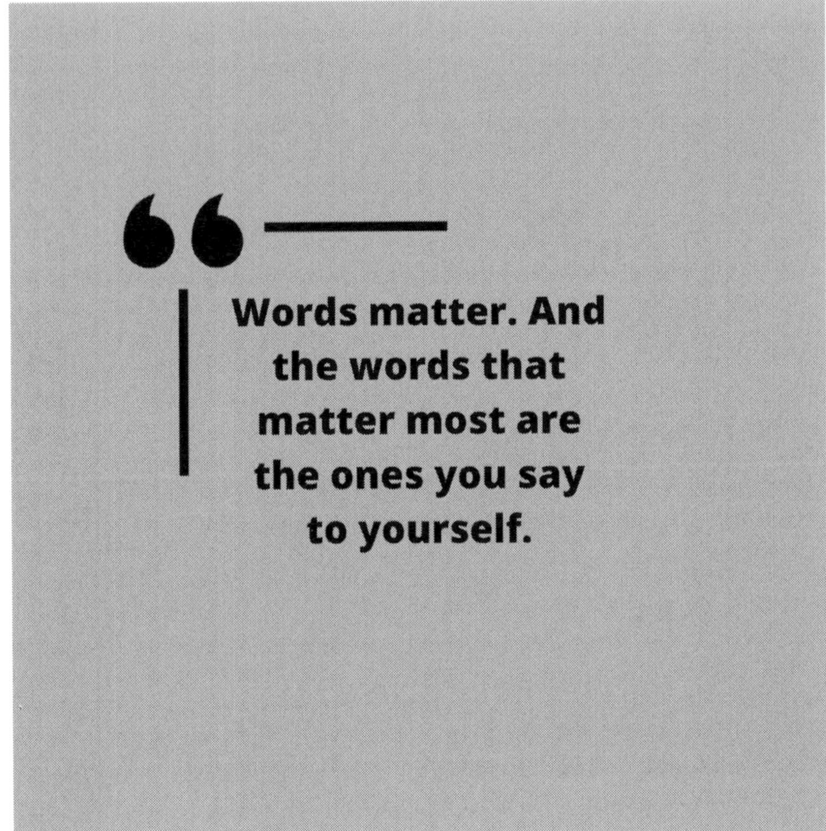
Words matter. And
the words that
matter most are
the ones you say
to yourself.

CHAPTER TWO
THE HEART OF PERFORMANCE

"Your values define who you are. Make them the fuel that propels you towards greatness."
LeBron James

Emily is a 20-year-old rising star in basketball, known for her exceptional skills and natural talent on the court. Coaches and teammates alike recognize her as a promising player with tremendous potential. She can execute impressive plays, sharply sink three-pointers, dribble past defenders effortlessly, and make critical assists that leave spectators in awe.

However, there's a frustrating element that accompanies Emily's undeniable talent. She often finds herself wrestling with inconsistency in her performance. One day, she's on fire, dominating the game and making it seem effortless. Her shots are impeccable, and her defensive maneuvers are top-notch. But when everyone expects her to maintain that level of excellence, she encounters moments of subpar play that leave her frustrated and her coach searching for answers.

Emily's inconsistency can be confounding, not only for her but for those who watch her play. It is not a lack of skill or dedication that holds her back, but her performance has a mysterious ebb and flow. She's determined to unlock the secret to consistently maintaining her peak level of play and is relentlessly pursuing understanding to overcome these fluctuations. Emily's journey in basketball is a familiar story of a young athlete grappling with the label of being "consistently inconsistent" in a sport she loves.

Moving forward, our focus will shift to the critical skill of goal setting, a pivotal phase in Emily's journey. Recognizing her exceptional talent and dedication, Emily's struggle with inconsistency in her basketball performance has become apparent. Mastering the art of effective goal setting is the key to providing Emily with a structured roadmap that addresses her peaks and valleys in performance. It propels her towards sustained excellence on the court. Setting clear and achievable goals will empower Emily to navigate the challenges of her varying performances, offering a strategic approach to enhance her skills and elevate her game to new heights. Through exploring goal-setting strategies and insights, we aim to equip Emily with the tools she needs to unlock her full potential and establish a more consistent and formidable presence in basketball.

Emily's experience is not an isolated one. Many athletes are deeply ingrained in the belief in the significance of setting goals. However, it's not uncommon to witness athletes grappling with the challenge of setting goals in a way that genuinely propels them toward success. Traditional goal setting unquestionably has its merits and is a valuable tool for many teams and athletes. I'm not here to dissuade you from using it if it works for you. Instead, I'd like to introduce an alternative perspective. What if there's another way to navigate the conventional goal-setting process? Let's embrace curiosity and delve deeper into this concept, exploring the pivotal role of values in charting a clear course to success.

Values function like the beam of a lighthouse, illuminating the path ahead and showing you the way. My experience has been that athletes with a firm understanding of their values quickly discover the advantages of doing so. When your values are crystal clear and integrated into your decision-making within your sport, the choices become markedly simpler. For example, if discipline is one of your core values as an athlete, you will only consider your training session complete if you have adhered to the prescribed weights program. This commitment to discipline takes precedence over any shortcuts or compromises, regardless of whether anyone is watching. Similarly, if you know you nicked the ball in cricket, even if the umpire missed it, your commitment to the value of honesty will guide your actions, and you'll walk. The lighthouse beams forth the honesty signal, and you'll be compelled to follow it.

Modifying the traditional goal-setting approach involves recognizing and aligning your values with your training, competition, and life beyond your sport. While it may seem straightforward to identify your values and consistently act by them, this process can be more challenging than it sounds. Many individuals struggle to articulate and pinpoint their values when prompted.

Can you easily name your core values?

Reflect on how you responded to that question. Did your values effortlessly come to mind, or did you find yourself tempted to mention socially esteemed values, perhaps to sound good, even if only to yourself? Alternatively, was your mind blank, leaving you uncertain about how to name your values, even though you know you have them? While it might be a simple task for some, let's revisit Emily's story to explore how her approach could offer valuable insights for you.

Navigating how Emily and I integrated her values into her preparation for the upcoming season was a thoughtful and individualized process. There are many different ways to identify one's values, and it's important to recognize that there isn't a one-size-fits-all method. We all possess an inherent understanding of our values, even when articulating them proves challenging. Emily's experience mirrored this common struggle; as we initiated the conversation, she sensed her values' direction but was cautious about voicing values that felt more like what she "should say" rather than what truly resonated with her. Emily's hesitation emphasized a pivotal aspect of this exploration: the exercise is futile if your values lack authentic alignment with your beliefs, thoughts, and behaviors. In essence, it's more beneficial to abstain from the process than to engage in a superficial expression of values that don't genuinely reflect your core principles.

DEFINING YOUR VALUES

In this chapter, I'll present my preferred method for defining personal values. This approach entails an extensive list featuring 120 values, each written on a separate piece of paper and arranged neatly on a table. The initial step involves swiftly sorting these values into two categories: those that resonate with you and those that don't connect as much. From the values that resonate, the challenge lies in whittling them down to a maximum of 20, or even fewer if feasible, through a deliberate selection process. Later in this chapter, I'll delve into the detailed step-by-step breakdown of this method, guiding you through each step. Ultimately, the objective is to distill your values into a concise 4–6 that authentically mirror your core beliefs. This approach is the method I followed with Emily. Upon completing this exercise, Emily meticulously honed her list of her top four values. We were certain she had pinpointed those values that best defined her because, after our thorough work, she leaned back in her chair, nodded, and, with a smile, affirmed, "Yes, that's me."

Identifying your values is an important step. What you do next is equally as important. People who live consistently with their values feel happier, more motivated, and more aligned with their purpose. The secret sauce to getting values working well for you is weaving them into your daily life and building them into your training and performance. Emily identified one of her values as consistency. In our discussions, she noted she is happiest when she feels she has control over her life. When talking about consistency, it made sense to her as a value as applying herself consistently to her tasks helped her to feel organized, and she was "ticking the boxes" of preparation for performance. The importance of consistency prompted our following conversation, "what does consistency look like in Emily's life?"

Her answers included:

- going to bed at the same time
- a bedtime routine (including packing her training bag for the next day)
- waking up at 5 am every day
- consistency in eating breakfast (although it didn't need to be the same meal)
- pre-hab routine when arriving at the courts
- extras after training
- two hours of university study each day (in addition to any lectures)

The completed list was around 20 tasks—all things that Emily wanted to include within each day, all achievable targets, and all behaviors that would assist her basketball. The critical focus we had for Emily with this list of tasks was the understanding that each time one of these was undertaken, she was satisfying her value of consistency. This elevated the importance of going to bed from simply a behavior to the affirmation of living according to her values.

Values are fundamental, and living a life consistent with those values is even more helpful. Importantly, the conversation around values became part of our regular weekly catchups. Initially, that conversation took some prompting by me, "Emily, tell me how your values have been part of your week?" But by the end of the season, I didn't need to ask the question. Personal values were so "front of mind" for Emily that she would start talking about them as part of her weekly review without my prompting. Her values became part of her daily reflections. She described herself as feeling more in control of her daily activities, and further, being mindful of how her values helped in her decision-making.

The connection was reaffirmed for Emily through the season. Unsurprisingly, consistency is a frequently desired outcome in sports, so the value of consistency was not just a mindset but an observable behavior. Emily received feedback from her coaches on her consistency (and reliability). She received more court time as her coaches became more confident of what she could achieve. By season's end, she was a regular starter. Her efforts were also noticed in the representative space, with selection in the National Team.

Living a life that aligns with your values provides comfort and confidence. Take Janet, a swimmer who holds honesty as one of her core values. Recently, when her strength and conditioning coach asked if she had completed her mobility exercises (which she had not), Janet found herself in a dilemma. Faced with the competing values of honesty and agreeableness, she panicked in the moment and falsely claimed she had done the exercises. This clash between her values and actions created a "mental rub"—the discomfort arising from believing in one thing and acting in contrast to that belief. In psychological terms, this phenomenon is called cognitive dissonance, where we "talk the talk" but fail to "walk the walk." Consider the following examples:

I'm reliable . . . But I just arrived late for a meeting.

I'm kind . . . But I just excluded someone from the group.

I am a leader . . . But I didn't speak up in the team when something needed to be said.

I'm curious . . . But I refused to consider someone else's point of view.

Acting against our values is a common behavior in human

psychology. The psychological discomfort in doing so can present as internal conflict, emotional distress, or a sense of moral unease, as it creates a discrepancy between our behavior and our deeply held convictions. Cognitive dissonance serves as a small piece of sandpaper in our minds, causing friction between our desires and our actions. By delving into your values and staying mindful of their influence on your life, you can sidestep cognitive dissonance by consistently aligning your behavior with those values. This approach not only helps you avoid internal conflict but also increases the likelihood of achieving greater happiness and moving closer to your goals.

Given the benefit of understanding and behaving consistently with our values, what place does goal setting have in sport? Is it time to step away from goal setting?

No! When done well, goal setting is an essential element for many athletes and teams. The research on the impact of goals on performance is undisputed. A mountain of research exists supporting the beneficial outcomes of setting goals. What I encourage you to consider before setting goals is to understand the role of your values in guiding your behavior. Your values and goals can work together to help you achieve your desired results. See your values as the beams from the lighthouse and your goals as the landmarks and parts of the ocean the light shines upon.

WHAT ARE YOUR VALUES?

If you are encouraged by Emily's focus on values, consider this for yourself. Where do you start? Here are a few questions to get you thinking about your values.

What words come to mind when you think of your values?

- Accountability
- Accuracy
- Achievement
- Belonging
- Boldness
- Challenge
- Curiosity
- Discipline
- Excitement
- Fun
- Growth
- Honesty
- Intelligence
- Intuition
- Joy
- Leadership
- Positivity
- Prudence
- Resourcefulness
- Results-oriented
- Self-control
- Spontaneity
- Success
- Teamwork
- Understanding
- Vitality

What are the behaviors you do/would need to do that would be consistent with those values?
If someone behaves against your values (e.g., Your value is honesty, and you witness someone tell a lie), how does that affect you? What do you think? How do you feel? What do you do?

A reliable test to determine the accuracy of your identified values is to consider how you respond when someone contradicts those values. When their behavior goes against what you hold dear, it serves as a litmus test for the authenticity of your values. For instance, if you regard leadership as a crucial value and observe another leader remaining silent when they should speak up, your thoughts and emotions in response to this action will reveal the true importance of leadership in your life.

In general, our values tend to fall into one of three distinct life domains:

Community and cultural values embody a community or culture's overarching principles. For example, your culture may prioritize hard work, spiritual faith, or group solidarity. Although you may resonate with these values to some extent, they may only partially mirror your convictions.

Role-related values are often established by external authorities to guide the conduct of a specific group, such as the values upheld in your workplace or on a board where you hold a position. They serve as a framework for responsibilities, and consistent adherence to them may be expected and monitored by others. To thrive in a particular role, you'll need to resonate with these values to some degree, even if you don't hold each one as closely as the others. Challenges may arise in environments like the workplace when the organization or its systems need to practice what they prescribe. This discrepancy is not uncommon, and I've observed it frequently in sporting teams, government organizations, and large corporations.

Core values encapsulate the essence of your individuality. They mirror your convictions and profoundly influence your choices and actions, helping you discern what is right and what is not. Core values are deeply ingrained, holding significant importance to your identity. Clarity about your values is crucial for personal satisfaction and significantly influences your overall performance.

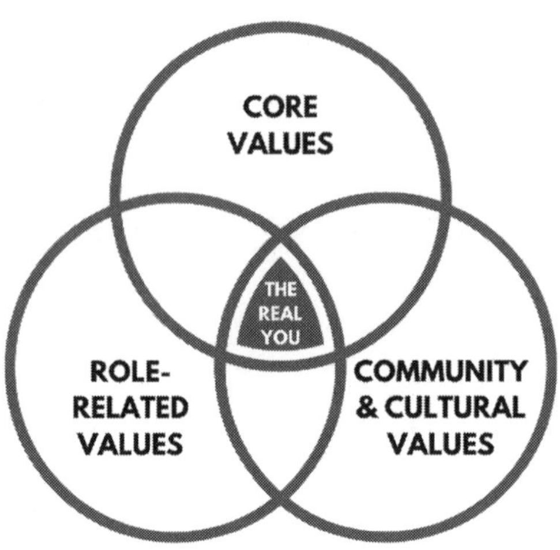

SETTING INDIVIDUAL VALUES

When I work with individuals on personal values, I like to hand them an envelope containing 120 small pieces of paper, a value written on each. To do the exercise, scan the QR code or click here, and a list of the values will be emailed to you.

Print the list, cut the page into individual words, and follow the steps below:

1. With the words in a pile before you, quickly sort them into two piles—the words that instantly resonate with you (a maximum of 20-25 words) in one pile and the remainder in the other.
2. Put the discarded words to one side.
3. Arrange the 20–25 words in front of you on the table.
4. Now, reduce the list to 3–5 words maximum.
5. Place the leftover words to one side.

You now have the 3–5 words that may resonate for you as your values. With these in mind, ask yourself:

- *How do I feel about these values as my core values?*
- *Do they describe "the real me" or "the me I wish to be?"*
- *What would be examples of things you would do that are consistent with the values?*
- *What would be examples of the things you would not do that are consistent with the values?*
- *How do those values get you closer to your goals and aspirations?*

The most significant resistance I hear from people doing this exercise is a reluctance to narrow the values down to 3–5 words. Remember that not choosing a value, e.g., "Determination," does not mean that being determined isn't important to you, nor something you don't do. Instead, 3–5 other values take a higher value for you, which is OK! You don't want a list of 10 values because you won't be able to hold them all front of mind and readily use them in your everyday life.

When I initially engaged in the personal values exercise, I habitually jotted down the four values at the top of a fresh page every time I embarked on a new project or significant task. I would then reflect on how I could use these values in the work I was about to tackle. These values were my guiding beacons, helping me determine the path forward. This practice enabled me to approach each task with a clear sense of purpose. With my values firmly aligned, I discovered a newfound motivation that, in my belief, led to improved performance on every occasion. It's been a while since I first undertook this exercise, and now these values are so deeply ingrained in my mind that I no longer need to reference the words explicitly. They have become an integral part of my mindset.

I found this particularly useful for tasks I needed more motivation to do. When you encounter something you don't want to do, think about how that task may align with your values. How might your values strengthen by doing the task? What will completing the task free you up to do next? Values-based behaviors are more motivating than those that don't align with our purpose.

While my values are somewhat irrelevant when you are considering your own, I am happy to share how I utilize them daily. I finalized four critical values for my professional work when I did the envelope exercise. I added an adverb to each value so that the action to go with it was front of mind. My four values are:

1. Complex ideas, simply messaged
2. Growth from understanding
3. Inherently grateful
4. Outrageously efficient

These values make sense to me. They are consistent with my aim when working on a project. As a side note, I often notice people's eyebrows raise when I share my value of being outrageously efficient. Why the phrasing? Well, let's face it: who wants to be organized? We all do, but the work behind it is often the work we don't want to do. Have you ever noticed the buzz you get when you clean out your car or finish tasks that have sat on your to-do list for a while? That dopamine hit kicks in whenever you complete something on your mind. The phrasing, to be outrageously efficient, is motivating for me. I love that dopamine hit, and the phrasing is a way to get excited about things like cleaning out my inbox (okay, excited might be a stretch—but I am a fan of zero inbox!).

UNDERSTAND YOUR VALUES BEFORE SETTING GOALS

So, if you've uncovered your values, are goals your next step? Not necessarily. Goal setting is an important foundation for most athletes and teams I have worked with, however, some athletes prefer to focus solely on their values. Then, their goal setting is used to apply to the competition. That combination can work well. Following your values through the season/competition phase might be enough. You can set your goals for the specifics of your craft.

What pointers would I offer for effective goal setting? Goal setting done well has several steps. I will outline them here, then provide an example of an individual athlete, Miranda, as well as a team, The Blazers, to illustrate the steps.

1. *Know what you want to achieve.*
What will success look like? What ***exactly*** are you wanting to achieve?

2. *Have you previously attained the goal?*
If yes, firstly—well done! Now, think about how that happened. Remember, *success leaves clues*. What was in place that set you up for success?
If not, why not? Is it a lack of opportunity? Haven't previously had the skill required? Was there information that you needed to know?

3. *What will be the markers of progress?*
Knowing you are improving and progressing is physically/tactically

necessary and psychologically motivating. How can you ***measure*** the progress you are making?

4. Is the goal within reach?
Perhaps you are returning from injury, or have just had a long season — maybe you have had some time away from your sport, or perhaps the goal you are setting is within your reach, but just not now. "Reach goals" are important. Think of a can up on a shelf slightly above what you can access with both feet on the ground. Lifting onto your toes, you grab the can. That is a reach goal. It is the goal that extends you. But look much higher above the shelf and see a third shelf, a foot above the shelf you just accessed. It also has a can on the rack. However, it's out of reach. No matter how high you reach, you'll never get there. Setting goals needs to be about extending ourselves within what is possible; it must be ***attainable***. If it isn't, it will likely only dishearten you when you don't reach it.

5. When do you intend the goal to be achieved?
This week, this month, this year? Goals without a deadline are not much more than a dream. Setting a ***timeframe*** for your goals introduces the pressure (and motivation) of an endpoint.

6. What is your assessment of the performance, and what will you do next?
The timeline has passed—how did you go? ***Evaluate*** the performance, considering what went well and where future improvements can be made. Evaluating brings closure to a goal and a useful ***reset*** point for setting the next goal.

Miranda (Cyclist)

1. *Know what you want to achieve.*
Miranda is a promising track cyclist and is hoping to perform well enough in her next competition to get selected in the national squad.

2. *Have you previously attained the goal?*
No. Miranda hasn't trialed at this level before. She's excited to trial and feeling nervous.

3. *What will be the markers of progress?*
Miranda's coach is pleased with her progress and her times in training sessions are looking promising.
They consider all aspects of her training and set:
* Specific lifting targets in the gym
* Cross training sessions to be completed
* Distances to be ridden
* Training sessions set by the coach
* Nutrition requirements
* Routine, including sleep time and journaling

4. *Is the goal within reach?*
Yes

5. *When do you intend the goal to be achieved?*
In 3 months' time at National Championships.

6. *What is your assessment of the performance, and what will you do next?*
Miranda performed well at Nationals but didn't complete her time trial with a fast enough time to qualify. She was disappointed with non-selection, but happy with a personal best time.
Miranda took a break for a few weeks and then after a review with her coach, reset to achieve the goal the following season.

Blazers (College Basketball Team)

1. *Know what you want to achieve.*
The Blazers have won the championships for the last two seasons. This year they want to achieve the "three-peat."

2. *Have you previously attained the goal?*
Yes, and the team are going into the team as favorites to win again this season. The team are certainly capable of winning, even with changes in team members for both the Blazers and their opposition.

3. *What will be the markers of progress?*
* The coach sets the season into 4 mini-seasons.
* The team values are reviewed, and the expectations are set around acceptable behaviors.
* Each training session is set by the coach.
* The strength coach sets a gym program for players to complete.
* The leadership group conduct reviews and feedback to the coaches.
* Once the general season is over the finals series becomes a reset point and the planning will recommence.

4. *Is the goal within reach?*
Yes

5. *When do you intend the goal to be achieved?*
Date of the Grand Final.

6. *What is your assessment of the performance, and what will you do next?*
Success! In a tough grand final, the Blazers narrowly beat the Hawks by 2-points. The post-season review indicated that half of the team would leaving for college next year. The coach re-signed for the next year and the team reset their goals with a focus to see how their new dynamic would work before setting any outcome goals.

Specific, Measurable, Attainable, Realistic, and Time-Based. Most athletes are familiar with SMART goals principles to set their goals. And I would certainly agree with those as a great framework. If you read back through my six tips above, you'll find a reference to each of the SMART principles highlighted ***with bold font***:

The message is the same while mine are written in a slightly different order. In addition to SMART, I like to add "ER," Evaluating and Resetting, to complete the cycle.

Here is a template for you to use for your next goal-setting activity.

1. *Know what you want to achieve.*

2. *Have you previously attained the goal? How? Why not?*

3. *What will be the markers of progress?*

4. *Is the goal within reach?*

5. *When do you intend the goal to be achieved?*

6. *What is your assessment of the performance, and what will you do next?*

As we wrap up this chapter, I want to stress the importance of diving deep into your values and mastering the art of goal setting. Emily's journey highlights the crucial role these elements play in your athletic path. Your values act like a compass, guiding your actions. Think of them as your true north, showing you the way to consistent performance and personal fulfillment. When you set goals, use the SMART principles, and add evaluation (E) and resetting (R) steps. Make these goals more than targets; let them reflect your core beliefs.

Journal prompt

Your inner coach is your ally in this journey. Use your journal to turn your values and goals into actionable plans.

Through your journal allow your thoughts to become a roadmap for aligning values with actions.

Stay consistent, sync your actions with values, and regularly review and adjust your goals as your beliefs evolve.

Use the foundational pillars discussed in this chapter to explore how your values fit in.

Let this reflection be your fuel, pushing you toward an authentic, purpose-driven performance.

Keep exploring, refining, and integrating your values into your athletic journey, step-by-step.

TRUST THE PROCESS.

CHAPTER THREE
SHARPENED CURIOSITY

"The only way to achieve greatness is to stop asking for permission."
Michael Phelps

JACINTA WAS no stranger to the intense world of competitive sports. As the coach of the formidable volleyball team, the Ace Avengers, she had seen her fair share of ups and downs on the court. They were a tight-knit group of athletes who had honed their skills together over time, and their camaraderie was as strong as their spike serves.

On this day, the stakes were high. The season's final game was underway, and a victory would secure their place as the league favorites, sending them into the much-coveted finals. The Avengers had a reputation for their precision and finesse, and they knew they had the potential to emerge victorious.

Yet, uncharacteristic mistakes were beginning to creep into their gameplay. Two consecutive silly errors had cost them valuable points, and the tension in the air was palpable. The crowd's expectations and the weight of their aspirations caused a momentary lapse in their otherwise flawless performance.

As the team gathered for a time-out, Jacinta could see the unease in the eyes of her players. It was clear that their minds had wandered, dwelling on the pressure of the moment and the anticipation of the result. It was at this juncture that Jacinta decided to utilize a lesson based on mindfulness.

"Listen up," Jacinta began, her voice steady and calm. "I know the stakes are high. But remember, the game is won one point at a time. We can't change the past, but we can control our actions in the present."

Jacinta looked each of her players in the eye, emphasizing her point. "As you stand in this huddle, keep your head where your sneakers are. I repeat, keep your head where your sneakers are. Focus on the now, the next serve, the next set, and the next spike. Be fully present in this moment, and the rest will follow. Let's play our game and win it point by point."

Jacinta's words were important. She knew that many of her players' minds had wandered. Some would be reliving previous mistakes, and others might worry ahead if the outcome doesn't go their way. It was her best chance of not getting them to think too far ahead by anchoring their thinking to something in the present. Success in sports is mastered by keeping your head in the right place at the right time. When you can match your thinking correctly to the future (planning a play), the past (learning from a mistake), or in the moment (executing a shot), you get the maximum amount of attention required for the task. Let's explore how you can do the same.

ENTERING THE TARDIS

During my childhood, one of my favorite television programs was the iconic series, "Doctor Who." Spanning decades, it captivated audiences with the adventures of the enigmatic Doctor, accompanied by various companions, including the ever-reliable robot dog, K9. With his time machine, the TARDIS, he traversed the vast expanse of time, bravely facing challenges to safeguard the universe. I recall watching the TARDIS materialize on screen, wishing to embark on similar escapades. Yet, what if I revealed that, in a sense, we each possess our own TARDIS-like potential?

I'd like you to think back and recall what you ate for breakfast (I hope you ate breakfast!)—what did you eat? Where were you when you were eating it? What did it taste like? Did you take some time and sit at a table? Or was it breakfast on the run?

Now let's shift our attention forward and think about what you'll be doing in eight hours' time. Will you be at work? At training? Spending time with family? Asleep? Imagine yourself in that environment and see yourself in that space. See if you can generate the feeling of being there.

Now, take in the environment you are in. Look up from your page (or tablet) and notice the features of where you are reading this book. Are you sitting/standing/lying? Is the temperature warm or cool? Is the lighting bright, or is it dim? Are you inside or outside?

Well done, you have just demonstrated the ability of humans to think across the three dimensions of time: the past, present, and future. Like a superpower, you can transport yourself as far forward or back in time as you wish: tomorrow, ten years' time, yesterday, or when you were five years old. Our mind can move backward and forward as it wanders or as we consciously think of ourselves in that direction.

Let's try now with your body. Mentally transport your body back to yesterday morning. Any luck? What about into the future, starting at 6 pm tomorrow? Sadly, our superpowers only stretch so far! Whilst seemingly a limitation, the reality that our bodies can only be in the present moment is important for our sporting performance.

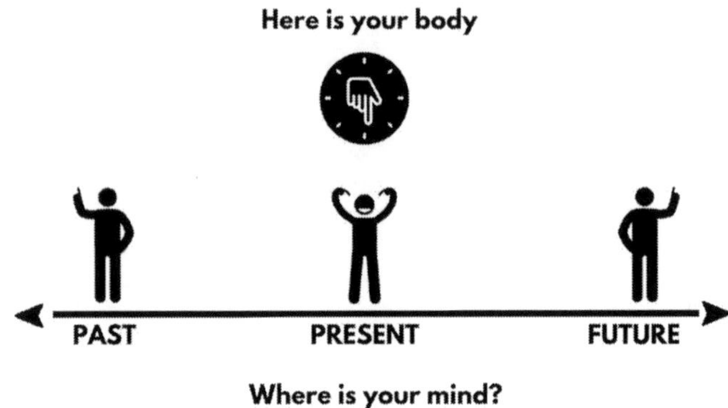

Keep your head in the *right* place at the *right* time

The relationship between the mind and body through time may sound abstract, but it has practical implications for performance. Importantly, it can be the difference between winning and losing. Mentally, you can transport your thinking forward, backward, and in the current moment (the present). The challenge for you to maximize your performance is to have your head in the right place at the right time. You may have heard it said that you must keep your awareness in the moment, like Jacinta's advice to keep your head where your sneakers are—and that is predominantly true in sports. Performance happens in the now. However, success comes from strategically switching thinking between the past, the future, and what is happening right now.

TIMELESS TOOLS FOR NAVIGATING THOUGHTS

Imagine a swimmer standing on the blocks about to start a swimming race: it will help the swimmer to have their thinking predominantly in the present—being aware of themself on the blocks, steadying their start stance, listening to the officials, and being ready to accelerate upon the gun. This is not the time to think about the pacing in the third lap or finishing with hands on the wall.

A footballer is in an offensive play with an opposition player running towards him at speed. The player's efforts need to be on maneuvering through the play. This is not the time to think about a defensive error from 10 minutes ago.

High performance requires your head to be in the right place at the right time. Does that mean you should always aim to have your head in the present moment? Often, is a better answer than always. While performing and competing, most of the time, it will help you to be focused on what you are doing in the given moment. This doesn't mean that whilst training or competing, there is no place for your thinking to look back to what has happened or ahead to future moments.

The sprinter may be in the first lap of their 800m track race, with a focused determination to maintain impeccable form. As the race progresses, her attention becomes finely attuned to her own performance and her competitors' strategies, analyzing the subtle changes in pace. This strategic awareness helps her recall the conversation with her coach about her race plan and execute a well-timed surge that can make all the difference in the later stages of the race.

The basketball point guard may carry the ball down the court as they glance at the clock to see 38 seconds remaining in the quarter, triggering a momentary shift in their thoughts. In this critical juncture, their mind quickly revisits the coach's instructions from the last time-out, guiding them on how to orchestrate the play and capitalize on the precious seconds left on the clock to make a game-changing move.

Further, athletes often need to fluidly transition between all three dimensions of time to excel in their performance. A prime illustration of this mental dance can be found in the sport of golf. Let's take the scenario of teeing off on the 3rd hole as an example. The golfer's mind effortlessly meanders through these temporal passages. First, they think back to the past, recalling the details of their previous experiences on this hole, the club choice and the success of their previous shots. Then, they turn their gaze to the future, envisioning where they want their shot to land as they peer down the fairway. Finally, their focus returns to the present moment, zeroing in on the ball resting on the tee. With a deep breath, they vividly visualize the shot they're about to execute, and, with absolute presence, tee off. This seamless orchestration of past, present, and future is a hallmark of their mental prowess.

The capacity of an athlete to adjust their mindset over time reflects a firm understanding of *time orientation*. Nevertheless, under the duress of high-pressure scenarios, athletes are susceptible to becoming stuck in a specific timeframe. This fixation can introduce distractions, significantly impairing their performance. For instance, imagine a golfer standing at the tee, mere seconds from swinging their club, plagued by thoughts like, "I hope I don't hook it again like last week." Such mental rigidity can be a performance hindrance, emphasizing the importance of mastering time orientation in sports psychology.

Unlocking the benefits of time orientation begins with a simple but powerful concept: understanding how the different passages of time can work in your favor within your sport. For those like me who enjoy the challenges of long-distance running, let's consider a few scenarios. Once we're done, it will be your turn!

REFLECTING ON PAST EXPERIENCES

Rainy race ahead: Imagine checking the weather forecast before your upcoming race and discovering a rainy day on the horizon. Suddenly, your mind drifts back to that last wet race you ran. You remember how competitors rushed to discard their raincoats just before the start while you shivered in the cold. This time, you're wiser and better prepared - your raincoat is packed.

Strategic running: In the final stages of a half marathon, a familiar competitor draws level with you, with 1 mile remaining. Memories of a previous encounter resurface, where she initiated a premature sprint, and you followed suit, only to falter in the final stretch. This recollection helps you resist the temptation to adopt someone else's race strategy and stay true to your own pace.

Fueling for success: As you approach the hydration station during the race, you vividly recall a previous race where you expertly managed your hydration and nutrition. You maintained your physicality with well-timed sips of water, replenishing electrolytes, and a much-needed bite of watermelon. Now, with that memory, you confidently navigate the station, ensuring you continue to fuel your body effectively for a successful race ahead.

THINKING IN THE PRESENT

Breath and cadence: During a long-distance run, there's a rhythm in every breath and a familiar cadence in every step. Breathing in sync with each stride is like creating a determination, anchoring oneself to the present moment, regardless of what lies ahead. When people speak of the "meditative" nature of running, it is about the ability to be in the present moment.

Sensory awareness: Exploring fresh running terrains, a runner connects with the present moment by fully immersing themselves in the sensory experience. The solid earth beneath their feet, the crisp touch of the breeze against their skin, and the natural beauty of their surroundings hold them in the here and now. It's not only a run; it's an expedition into the present moment.

Form and technique: With each stride, the path becomes an opportunity for focusing on form and technique. The runner does a body scan, carefully analyzing posture, subtly correcting their arm movements, and optimizing their stride, treating every step precisely. They are vigilant, safeguarding against potential missteps, all while savoring the enjoyment of running in the present, not dwelling on the distance covered or past races.

THINKING IN THE FUTURE

Tactical pacing: While in the early miles of a marathon, the runner thinks ahead to the final 10 miles. They calculate the pace required to achieve their target finish time and strategically adjust their speed. This forward-thinking approach ensures enough energy left in the tank to finish strong, maintaining a consistent and efficient pace throughout the race.

Milestone mile markers: The runner sets mental milestones for themselves during the race. The marathon is divided into segments and an approach is planned for each section. For instance, upon reaching the halfway mark, the runner reminds themself to stay steady and resist the temptation to push too hard. This future-oriented thinking keeps them grounded and determined, with sights firmly set on crossing the finish line successfully.

Sprint to the finish: Entering the final stretch of the marathon, the approach to the finish line is a clear visual. The runner mentally prepares to shift gears, increasing their pace for a strong finish. This forward-thinking strategy motivates the runner to give their all in those crucial last few miles, leaving nothing to chance and ensuring they end the race on a high note.

In running, success is not solely determined by the athlete's physical prowess but also by their mental acumen. Effective runners recognize that mastering the art of running requires a well-rounded approach encompassing past, present, and future thinking. Reflecting on past experiences and learning from them allows runners to fine-tune their strategies. Embracing the present moment through sensory awareness or form perfection ensures they are always at their best during each step of the race. Looking forward to the future keeps them goal-oriented and focused on achieving their dreams. Every sport can benefit from this understanding. There are always lessons offered in the past worth remembering and learning from. Thinking ahead into the future will help to adjust and adapt to the completion of the competition. Finally, thinking in the present moment will ensure you keep your thoughts as helpful as possible relating to your performance.

Now it's your turn. With space in this book for you to write your own examples (or use your journal), take a moment to consider how these strategies can be applied to your specific sport. Jot down 2–3 examples for each category—past, present, and future—tailored to your goals and aspirations. By doing so, you can harness the full power of your mind and propel your athletic performance to new heights.

Past:..

....

Present:...

....

Future:...

....

In high-performance sport, the ability to harness the power of past, present, and future thinking is a hallmark of those who continually push the boundaries of their achievements. However, while many athletes excel in strategizing for the future and learning from past experiences, the true challenge often lies in mastering the present moment—the "now." It's here, in the present, that races are won, goals are scored, personal bests are reset, and mental resilience is forged. Yet, for many, it can be a daunting task to keep your mind fully immersed in the present. The power to harness the present moment is within your grasp, and it's the very key to unleashing your true athletic potential.

The "now" is where your body and mind must come together, where each step, each breath, and each sensation matters. To sharpen your present-moment awareness, here are a few strategies you can employ:

Sport-specific drills: Incorporate sport-specific exercises and drills demanding full physical engagement. Whether it's perfecting your golf swing, practicing your free throws, or fine-tuning your tennis serve, these hands-on experiences in your chosen sport will sharpen your present-moment awareness and refine your athletic skills.

Active listening: Beyond sports, practice active listening in your daily interactions. When someone is talking to you, make a conscious effort to listen completely. Avoid letting your mind wander or planning your response in advance. Immerse yourself in their words and the emotions behind them. This skill enriches your personal relationships and sharpens your capacity for undivided attention. Your coach is a great person to practice this with!

Focused breathing: Dedicate brief moments during the day, perhaps 2–3 minutes, to focus solely on your breathing. Feel the air as it enters your nostrils, fills your lungs, and is expelled. This simple act of paying attention to your breath can serve as an anchor to the present moment. When the pressure mounts in a race, returning to this anchor can help you regain your composure and focus.

Remember, mastering the present moment is not an overnight feat, but consistent practice and patience can be a game-changer in your athletic journey. By elevating your present-moment awareness, you'll sharpen your focus, enhance your decision-making, and perform at your peak when it matters most. The *now* is where champions are made, and you have the power to achieve your potential.

Journal Prompt

How you can improve your ability to switch between the past, present and future.

Which of the skills above might you use to improve staying in the moment?

THE POWER OF WONDER

Imagine if I told you that there's a single word you can incorporate into your everyday conversations, a word that can transform your life in remarkable ways. It can help you stay focused on what truly matters, increase your chances of success, and even boost your intelligence. Sounds intriguing. Well, that word is ***curiosity***, and it's an absolute game-changer in the world of high performance!

In a memorable episode of the popular television series "Ted Lasso," we witness a captivating scene where Ted, an unlikely American coach of an English Premier League football team, engages in a high-stakes game of darts against the team's former owner, Rupert. At the outset, Ted intentionally projects an image of ineptitude in darts, luring Rupert into a significant wager, directly impacting Rebecca, Ted's boss, and Rupert's former spouse.

Initially, Ted's dart-throwing performance is subpar, reinforcing the impression of his inadequacy. However, with a mischievous grin, Ted humorously quips, "That's right, I forgot I'm left-handed." Surprisingly, he hit the bullseye, convincingly outplaying Rupert. During a subsequent monologue, Ted reveals a poignant facet of his life—his formative years spent playing darts alongside his father. This is a facet of Ted's character that Rupert could have discovered had he exhibited curiosity about Ted's background and interests.

What stands out most in this scene is Ted's insightful observation, "So I get back in my car, and I'm driving to work, and all of a sudden, it hits me. All of them fellas that used to belittle me, not one of them was curious. You know, they thought they had everything all figured out. So, they judged everything, and they judged everyone. And I realized that they were underestimating me . . . who I was had nothing to do with it. 'Cause if they were curious, they would've asked questions. You know? Like, 'Have you played a lot of darts, Ted?'" Ted throws another dart and hits his second triple 20 before continuing, "To which I would've answered, 'Yes, sir. Every Sunday afternoon at a sports bar with my father, from age 10 until I was 16 when he passed away.'"

Let's take a moment to delve into what curiosity truly means. When we talk about curiosity, we refer to that strong desire to learn or discover something new. Adopting a curious mindset opens your thinking, broadens your horizons, and encourages you to explore alternative viewpoints and fresh approaches. Curious individuals are the ones who ask questions, actively listen, seek knowledge, and embrace the possibility of uncharted territories.

The best part is that you don't need to be overly smart to be curious. However, cultivating curiosity will undoubtedly make you smarter!

There are many benefits of curiosity for athletes; here are some of my favorites.

1. When you are driven by curiosity, you will experience more enjoyment and engagement in your training and competition. Asking questions and wondering how to improve is a motivating mindset. You are, therefore, more likely to see change and improvement as a possibility rather than being stuck where you are. Combining the greater willingness to learn will improve your sports IQ. This improvement in intelligence has been shown in school students. A study conducted by neuropsychologist Adrian Raine and his colleagues examined the curiosity levels of three-year-olds. Upon retesting them at the age of 11, the study found that children who exhibited high curiosity at three years old showed a significant increase of 12 points in their intelligence test scores, eight years later compared to those who were less curious. Curiosity becomes a pathway to expand your understanding, and therefore increase your sporting intelligence.

. . .

2. A curious mindset can act like a volume control on your emotions. By exploring different perspectives and trying to find new alternatives, feelings of anger are reduced, and frustration becomes less, leading to a calmer temperament to improve decision-making. Curiosity makes you more mindful of your emotions, and therefore more in control to make changes about them.

3. In addition to reducing anxiety and worry, when you embrace curiosity, improved psychological well-being and overall satisfaction are common. Therefore, athletes who exhibit greater curiosity are more likely to report higher levels of happiness and gratitude. Within my book, *The Elite* I included a chapter on the science of gratitude. Not only does gratitude improve our wellbeing, but it is a powerful performance enhancer.

4. Curiosity is a feature of empathy. When someone is genuinely interested in connecting with others through conversations, they will be perceived by others as better teammates and nicer people! Whilst many athletes will respect a teammate for their physical prowess, we tend to have greater trust in those people that we like. Curiosity can put a skip in your step and make you more appealing to others. Taking the time to get to know others will influence how we are perceived, and curiosity can help us to get there. Curiosity can be a tool to form better relationships with our teammates and coaches.

5. Researchers have established a close connection between dopamine, the brain's reward neurotransmitter, and the state of curiosity in the brain. As you explore and satisfy your curiosity, your brain releases dopamine into your system, resulting in increased feelings of happiness. Helping your brain get to this physical state through curiosity will help you be more vigilant, adapt more quickly

to your environment, and function better when you encounter new challenges and opportunities for growth.

6. Studies conducted at the Curiosity Lab at Tel Aviv University indicate that simply mentioning the word "curiosity" in a sentence can have a notable impact on our energy levels and enhance our ability to learn. Describing a day when you felt curious has been shown to increase physiological arousal by 20% more than recounting a moment of profound happiness.

One of the initial barriers to being more curious is a lack of awareness. In our busy, modern lives, preoccupied with daily routines and the relentless demands of responsibilities, we often lose sight of the profound value of curiosity. Our obligations can obscure the path to asking questions, leaving little space to pause, reflect, and engage in meaningful conversations that fuel our curiosity. Yet, to rise to our full potential, mindfulness must be established as a foundational skill. Curiosity cannot thrive without it. We'll explore how to do that within this chapter.

COURAGE RISING: EMBRACING VULNERABILITY

The next foe we must confront is the fear of vulnerability. Imagine two athletes engaged in a conversation. One athlete speaks of a novel training tool, while the other stands at a crossroads. Do they let the fear of admitting their lack of knowledge halt the conversation, or do they embrace the opportunity to learn? Curiosity unfolds when the latter choice is made. They can discover new knowledge and personal advantage by asking questions and delving deeper into the subject. The humility of acknowledging one's limitations is a small price to pay for the wealth of insights gained. The notion of being experts in all domains is a mirage; curiosity bridges the gaps in our understanding.

The fear of failing, particularly in sports, can be a paralyzing force that prevents athletes from venturing into new territory. It discourages them from exploring new training methods, techniques, or strategies that may be key to improvement. This fear often stems from the pressure to perform, the desire to maintain a flawless track record, and the potential consequences of underachievement. Overcoming this fear is essential to unlock the full potential of curiosity within sports, as it's through experimentation and pushing boundaries that athletes can reach new heights.

Another formidable adversary that athletes encounter is the trap of narrow-mindedness. A rigid mindset and reluctance to consider alternative training methodologies can effectively shut the door to curiosity. Athletes who remain stubborn in their approach may resist change, hindering their adaptability to the ever-evolving landscape of sports techniques and strategies. To foster curiosity, athletes must embrace flexibility, open-mindedness, and a willingness to explore new methods. Through this openness, they can harness the power of curiosity to drive their growth and excellence in sports.

In the information-rich world of sports, athletes often find themselves drowning in an overwhelming sea of data, statistics, and training methodologies. The abundance of information can make distinguishing valuable insights from the less relevant challenging. Athletes must sift through this vast ocean of knowledge to find those pearls of wisdom to enhance their performance. Information overload, therefore, emerges as a significant barrier to curiosity-driven learning. To overcome this obstacle, athletes must develop critical thinking skills and discern the information that truly matters to their development. They must learn to focus on the knowledge that will propel them forward in their sporting journey.

Inequity in resource access is yet another hurdle that can obstruct athletes' path to curiosity. Some athletes have access to state-of-the-art training facilities, experienced coaching expertise, and cutting-edge technology, while others may be less fortunate. Social and cultural pressures often push athletes to conform to established norms, stifling their curiosity for innovative approaches. Past failures and criticisms can cast a long shadow, discouraging athletes from taking risks or experimenting with less conventional methods. Low self-esteem will understandably erode an athlete's curiosity and hinder personal growth.

To overcome these challenges, athletes can take practical steps to boost their confidence in tackling these barriers. Cultivating mindfulness, embracing vulnerability, and nurturing a performance mindset are essential strategies to help navigate the obstacles. By developing mindfulness, athletes can improve their self-awareness and learn to stay focused on the present moment, making understanding their limitations and strengths easier. Embracing vulnerability enables them to let go of the fear of not knowing and open themselves to new learning experiences. Nurturing a performance mindset instills the belief that challenges and setbacks are opportunities for growth and improvement.

Furthermore, athletes can draw strength from their intrinsic motivation, which keeps them moving forward. Intrinsic motivation, the innate desire to learn and explore, provides the energy and determination to overcome these formidable barriers. To foster curiosity in sporting athletes, providing a supportive environment where risk-taking, innovation, and learning is encouraged is crucial. Building athletes' self-confidence, offering access to relevant resources, and promoting a performance mindset are key strategies to overcome these barriers. With these practical tools and the power of intrinsic motivation, athletes can confidently progress in their journey, embracing curiosity as the key to unlocking their full potential in sports.

Curiosity truly is a remarkable trait. It can shape our lives, enhance our relationships, and elevate our intelligence. In the sporting domain, it can help us understand ourselves better, develop a smart game plan, and achieve our goals.

This thought-provoking moment underscores a valuable life lesson—the haste to pass judgment leaves little room for curiosity. While it's natural to eventually form conclusions, investing time in fostering curiosity is essential. Embracing curiosity enriches one's understanding, enabling better beliefs and performance.

THE KNOWLEDGE + CURIOSITY LOOP: INCREASING YOUR CURIOSITY MINDSET

A powerful feedback loop that combines knowledge and curiosity is the mindset strategy that can propel athletes to new heights of excellence. This loop resembles how a star quarterback refines his passing technique by constantly seeking knowledge and questioning what's possible. It's not just a theory; it's a game-changer for athletes, teams, and coaches who adopt it. So, let's venture into its essence and uncover how you can utilize this powerful mechanism to elevate your athletic performance to its peak.

The knowledge + curiosity feedback loop is the interplay between knowledge and curiosity. It begins with knowledge—understanding the sport, its intricacies, techniques, and strategies. As athletes acquire knowledge and deepen their understanding, a remarkable shift occurs. Curiosity awakens, igniting an innate desire to explore further, uncover hidden insights, and push the boundaries of their own abilities. Curiosity becomes the catalyst, fueling the athlete's quest for answers, encouraging them to seek alternative perspectives, and prompting the discovery of new information and innovative approaches. As athletes indulge their curiosity, actively seeking knowledge through various means, they gain a deeper comprehension of their sport, its nuances, and its growth potential.

This newfound knowledge, in turn, ignites even more curiosity within athletes. The more they learn, the more they realize there is still more to discover. This creates a self-reinforcing feedback loop where each step fuels the next, propelling athletes on a continuous learning, exploration, and improvement journey.

Imagine a passionate young tennis player, Jenna, eager to elevate her game to a professional level. Jenna begins by immersing herself in the sport, absorbing knowledge about different strokes, court strategies, and the game's physics. As she gains this foundational knowledge, her curiosity for improving is ignited.

Curiosity drives her to seek insights into tennis techniques, such as mastering the topspin forehand or perfecting the serve. Jenna reads books, watches videos, and consults with experienced coaches and players to gain a better understanding. This exploration fuels her curiosity even more.

With her curiosity heightened, Jenna starts experimenting with various strategies and techniques on the court. She tests her ideas, takes risks, and, in the process, discovers what works best for her playing style. This experimentation sparks new knowledge as Jenna learns from her successes and mistakes. Rather than being frustrated by errors, they are welcomed as the next step on Jenna's path.

As her game evolves, Jenna becomes more curious about the mental aspect of tennis—how to stay focused during high-pressure matches, read opponents, and strategize effectively. This curiosity leads Jenna to study sports psychology, attend mental training workshops, and engage in mental exercises, further enhancing her performance.

This continuous cycle of knowledge and curiosity propels the young tennis player to new heights. Jenna's game becomes more refined, her understanding of tennis more advanced, and her curiosity continues to fuel a quest for excellence. Jenna adopted the knowledge + curiosity feedback loop as a powerful tool that ensured a path of constant improvement, helping edge her closer to achieving the dream of becoming a professional tennis player.

The more I know, the more questions I have.

Now, let's delve into the actionable steps you can take to make the most of the knowledge + curiosity feedback loop in sports.

1. *Commit to a curious mindset:* Embrace a perspective of curiosity by approaching your sport with a sense of interest and a desire to learn. See challenges as opportunities for growth, constantly seeking to expand your understanding and push the boundaries of your abilities.
2. *Seek knowledge actively:* Take an active role in acquiring knowledge relevant to your sport. Engage in reading sports literature or watching videos, studying successful athletes, watching matches or competitions, and seeking guidance from coaches, trainers, or experts who can provide valuable insights.
3. *Ask insightful questions:* Develop the habit of asking thoughtful questions. Challenge conventional wisdom, seek clarification, and explore alternative viewpoints. By delving deeper into your sport, you gain a more comprehensive understanding and identify new areas for growth. Examples of insightful questions you can ask are at the end of this chapter.
4. *Embrace lifelong learning:* Recognize that learning in sport is a lifelong journey. Continuously seek opportunities to expand your knowledge and skills, both within your specific discipline and in complementary areas that can enhance your performance.
5. *Connect knowledge to practical applications:* Apply the knowledge you acquire to your training sessions and competitive performances. Seek to integrate different techniques, strategies, and approaches, adapting them to suit your style and objectives. Experiment with new training methods, explore innovative tactics, and constantly challenge yourself to push beyond your comfort zone. By bridging the gap between knowledge and application, you elevate your performance on the field.
6. *Reflect and evaluate:* Regularly reflect on your learning journey, evaluating the impact of acquired knowledge on your performance and overall development. Your journaling would be great for this.

Identify areas where further curiosity and knowledge can be applied, setting goals for continued growth and improvement.

By embracing the practical steps outlined above, athletes can tap into the immense potential of the knowledge + curiosity feedback loop. Athletes acquire valuable insights with each step, heighten their curiosity, and ignite a thirst for further knowledge. This perpetual cycle of learning and curiosity catalyzes continuous improvement, propelling athletes to new levels of performance, understanding, and fulfillment within their sport.

Embrace the power of the knowledge + curiosity feedback loop and unlock the untapped potential within your sporting journey. Let curiosity guide you on a remarkable path of discovery, growth, and excellence as you unravel the depths of your capabilities and redefine the boundaries of what you can achieve in your chosen sport.

Journal Prompt

Can you think of practical actions you can adopt to strengthen your curiosity? Spend some time with your inner coach thinking about the role of curiosity in your sport and journal some ideas about what might benefit you.

ADOPTING THE MINDSET OF THE CURIOUS OBSERVER

Ivan, a talented wheelchair rugby player, had always possessed the physical skills and athleticism necessary to excel on the court. However, he grappled with a mental aspect of the game that many players face—the challenge of overcoming self-doubt and pessimism in the face of mistakes. While thumbing through a sports psychology book, Ivan stumbled upon the concept of the "curious observer," a mental skill that intrigued him. This approach involved distancing oneself from errors, allowing for a more objective and curious perspective.

Eager to implement this concept, Ivan tried it during his next practice. Despite a misdirected pass that would have previously triggered frustration, he applied the curious observer technique. Taking a mental pause, he observed the situation with genuine curiosity, reframing the error as a puzzle to be solved rather than a failure. This shift in perspective marked a turning point for Ivan. Practicing with a curious mindset, he consistently asked himself, "What can I learn from this mistake, and how can I improve?"

Over time, Ivan noticed a significant improvement in his performance. The curious observer approach helped him forge a more constructive relationship with his mistakes. No longer dwelling on errors with self-judgment, he viewed them as opportunities for growth and learning. This mental space allowed him to explore new solutions and mindsets in the face of adversity.

Ivan's newfound mental skill became his secret weapon as the season progressed. Embracing each error with curiosity, he transformed his mindset, positively influencing his teammates with his composure and problem-solving abilities during challenging moments.

Ivan's journey with the curious observer technique expanded beyond the rugby court, becoming a valuable life lesson. It taught him that maintaining a curious and non-judgmental perspective in the face of mistakes was a path to growth, resilience, and continuous improvement. Ivan had unlocked a mental tool that elevated his game and enriched his approach to challenges both on and off the court.

The brilliance of the curious observer approach lies in providing a mental 'gap' between the error and the thinking process. This gap reduces judgment and criticism, fostering a mindset of curiosity and helpfulness. A helpful mindset proves more beneficial in steering individuals closer to success.

Developing a curious mindset involves asking thought provoking questions. Thinking the questions through and not being too quick to come to a definitive answer is all part of the curious mindset.

Journal prompt

Here are some examples of questions you could consider:

"What if . . ."

"Why not try . . ."

"How can we improve . . ."

"In what ways can we enhance . . ."

"Have you ever considered . . ."

"What's the potential of . . ."

"Can we push the boundaries of . . ."

"Is there a better approach to . . ."

"How might we innovate in . . ."

"What if we explored . . ."

"Are there opportunities in . . ."

"What's the hidden potential of . . ."

"Is there room for improvement in . . ."

"How can we challenge the norms of . . ."

"What new insights can we gain from . . ."

"Call me crazy, but how/why/when/what . . ."

THINK
OUTSIDE
THE BOX

CHAPTER FOUR
FROM FIXED MINDSET TO FLEXIBLE EXCELLENCE

"It's not about perfect. It's about effort. And when you bring that effort every single day, that's where transformation happens. That's how change occurs."
Jillian Michaels

WITHIN SPORT, it is not so much what happens to you but what you do about it that matters. In 2022, the Papua New Guinea Orchids, the National Women's Rugby League Team, competed in the highly contested World Cup in the United Kingdom. The team had not won a game in the previous World Cup campaign, and there was pressure and expectation on the team to perform well. I worked with the team in the months prior. We spent time in our base in Leeds, England, acclimatizing to the weather, food, hotel accommodation, and, for many, the first overseas trip. At the end of the second week, the team was to play a trial match in the nearby city of York. It was an evening game, and the weather was bitter. We left on the team bus to drive the 40 km to York with plenty of time, and then hit unexpected traffic delays. Arriving at the stadium with only half our planned preparation time in front of us, the team squeezed into a tiny change room—so small that most of the gear (and staff) had to be left outside the rooms. The team quickly changed; those who could get strapped did; one of our players had left her protective strapping back at the hotel. With only 10 minutes available, the team ran out, in the rain, onto the field for a shortened warm-up. The field was AstroTurf, not grass—a new surface for most of the team. The team lined up for the national anthem without the full normal warm-up. The tech in the stadium failed, and halfway through the anthem, the sound dropped out to silence, with the PNG anthem incomplete. With seemingly everything going wrong, fortunately, we had a mental strategy to deal with all these disruptions so it would not impact the game, which was about to commence.

Throughout my years, I've faced various challenges across all sports during competitive periods. These include transport delays, misplaced luggage, internal conflicts, defeats, gambling concerns, controversial referee decisions, accusations of foul play, crucial player injuries, sleep deprivation, disruptive roommates, team selection dilemmas, feelings of homesickness, inadequate facilities, player and coach dismissals, and instances of substance abuse. If there's an obstacle, it's likely crossed my path.

Certainly, one can take measures to mitigate certain risks:

- well-considered player selection
- contingency plans for team logistics
- discussions regarding team rules, values and expectations
- transparent communication among staff
- clear dialogue with players

However, despite the most diligent planning, unforeseen circumstances can arise. *It is how you choose to manage them that really matters.*

Avoiding challenges in sports is ultimately fruitless. Embracing the adversities encountered in sports should be encouraged, even if it initially seems a stretch. The key lies in swiftly acknowledging and embracing these challenges. I understand that embracing adversity might sound like a big ask, and I've encountered resistance from athletes regarding acceptance. My response to this resistance is simple: You don't have to enjoy the adversity, but acknowledging it is crucial. Acceptance grants you the mental space needed to move forward. Refusing to accept a situation will only entangle your thoughts in a futile mental battle, trapping you in denial.

How does one achieve acceptance and move forward? Is there a strategy to assist in acknowledging a situation and progressing beyond it? Could curiosity play a role in this process?!

FORTUNATELY/UNFORTUNATELY

Athletes are often advised to manage what they can control—a sound recommendation. Yet, frequently, athletes express uncertainty about how to execute this advice. In preparation for the World Cup, I introduced a favorite strategy of mine to both players and staff. This technique sets a gold standard for navigating what can be controlled, preventing athletes from getting tangled in elements where their influence is limited.

I liken this strategy to a mental game of tennis. It involves swiftly reframing a real or imagined situation by viewing its components through the lenses of "fortunately" and "unfortunately." Picture these as opposing sides of a tennis court, with "fortunately" on one side and "unfortunately" on the other. When life throws an "unfortunately," imagine it volleying over the net for "fortunately" to counteract it. Let's put this into context with an example.

Situation: You are traveling overseas with a large group of athletes.
Unfortunately: The flight has been delayed 5 hours.
Fortunately: You like duty-free shopping, and this is a chance to get to know your teammates better.
Unfortunately: You are seated in the center section of the plane, away from the wall (which is your preference).
Fortunately: That places you on the outside of the aisle so you can get up and down as you choose.
Unfortunately: When you arrive at your destination, your suitcase is lost.
Fortunately: You packed training gear in your carry-on luggage, and the bag will get to you eventually.
Unfortunately: You now have a 4-hour bus trip to get to your hotel.
Fortunately: You can rest on the bus and listen to your favorite music.

Backward and forward like a tennis match, the *fortunately/unfortunately* thinking strategy will give you the mental flexibility to manage any situation you or your team faces. The strategy is to take the undesired event or outcome and then reconsider it from a perspective of helpfulness.

How did the *fortunately/unfortunately* strategy come to the aid of the Orchids on that rainy night in York? Fortunately (see what I did there?!) we had diligently practiced this strategy in various scenarios during the two weeks leading up to the match. Consequently, when we arrived at the stadium, facing several formidable challenges, the team approached them with remarkable composure.

We had brainstormed some likely scenarios that may not go how we wanted, and on the evening of our first game, many of the challenges were exactly what we expected. Because we had practiced (and embraced) disappointment in our time together leading into the first game, as soon as the first adversity presented (the bus driver announced we were going to arrive later than planned), players were heard to call out through the bus "... but fortunately ..." and we were mentally ready to go. The high-performance team took charge and started strapping players on the bus, and the staff already on the ground got as prepared as they could prior to our arrival.

I stood, filled with admiration, as our team met every obstacle head-on, like water rolling off a duck's back. The squad lined up to face the home side and could have handled any challenge during this campaign. They consistently embraced challenges, seeking opportunities in every situation.

In their first game together as a squad, going up against the English Premier League team, they secured a convincing victory with an impressive score line. Despite the game's difficulties and the disappointing tournament-ending injury suffered by a key player, the team consistently demonstrated their ability to reframe adversity, leaving negativity behind and moving firmly into the future.

The *fortunately/unfortunately* technique offers a method for enhancing mental flexibility. Being rigid in your perspective of a situation hampers creative thinking and amplifies feelings of distress, worry, and anxiety when faced with setbacks. Moreover, dwelling on undesired outcomes can breed negativity, cascading into even more problematic consequences when encountering the next challenge. Engaging the *fortunately/unfortunately* technique helps shift your focus away from the unfavorable situation, offering a more constructive and advantageous perspective.

It's important to note that this strategy does not ask you to like the unfortunate situation, but it frees you from getting trapped in the cycle of its negativity. Finding a way to think "fortunately" around an event allows you to accept what has happened, reframe how you view it, and move on. It's a great way to control the uncontrollable and unfortunate things that can occur at the elite level.

A word of caution. While the outlined strategy is effective in many situations shortly after they unfold, certain sporting events (e.g., dismissal from a team or a career-ending injury) carry such weight that attempting a swift turnaround might appear unrealistic given their emotional gravity.

When confronted with such profound moments, it's natural to

undergo a period of grief. Allowing yourself to experience emotions like sadness, anger, disappointment, or distress is not just acceptable but expected—it's a fundamental part of the human response to these situations.

The question arises: Can the "fortunately" mindset apply to these challenging circumstances? The answer hinges on the situation. Over time, there might be an opportunity for a shift in perspective, but arriving there could take time. The essential takeaway is that when facing situations that halt you, it's crucial to treat yourself kindly, permit yourself to grieve if necessary, and contemplate the benefits for rethinking your outlook moving forward.

PERFECT IS THE ENEMY OF EXCELLENCE

Think of your sporting role models. Picture them during a grueling training session—working at their craft, honing their skills. Do they make mistakes? Of course, they do; in fact, I hope so!

A common phrase in high performance is, "Perfect is the enemy of good." It means that the pursuit of perfection can obstruct progress and hinder achieving great results. When striving for perfection, the focus can be so intent on achieving an unattainable ideal that we lose sight of what can be achieved, and the only outcome will be disappointment. This can lead to frustration, indecision, and often, inaction.

For example, if a writer spends too much time trying to make a perfect first draft, they may never finish the manuscript. Or, if a manager tries to create an ideal plan, they may become so bogged down in the details that they never put the strategy into action.

Athletes are no exception to this reality. The constant expectation of perfection can leave no room for any performance to be deemed satisfactory. Athletes with perfectionist tendencies frequently find themselves in a state of perpetual disappointment. Moreover, the inner coach accompanying the relentless pursuit of perfection is often negative, unconstructive, and detrimental to confidence.

So, if not perfection, then what should we aim for?

Prioritizing progress and doing our best with the resources and information is more beneficial than chasing an unattainable ideal. Instead of focusing on perfection, I encourage you to consider what excellence means. Pursuing excellence is not only achievable but also highly motivating. Focusing on excellence will spur you into action more so than aiming for perfection.

For athletes, pursuing perfection is often a misguided endeavor, leading them down a path where the unattainable becomes the adversary of the attainable. We envision flawless performances, impeccable execution, and achievements that leave no room for critique. However, it's essential to acknowledge the impossible nature of perfection. While it's a noble aspiration, it often exists as a distant star, forever out of reach. Legendary producer of Saturday Night Live, Lorne Michaels, captured this sentiment brilliantly when he stated, "I say it every week: We don't go on because we're ready. We go on because it's 11:30 pm." This message also resonates in sports—there's an inherent truth that it's not about being perfectly prepared but about being ready-enough when the time demands it.

Similarly, athletes must understand that "perfect" is a fickle benchmark. Instead, I encourage a shift in focus to achieving excellence. Striving for excellence entails meticulous preparation, dedicated training, and a commitment to honing one's skills. It's a goal that stands firmly within the realm of achievability. Excelling doesn't mean error-free; it means pushing boundaries, surpassing previous limits, and consistently delivering performances that reflect dedicated effort.

Let's face it—rarely does anyone step onto the field, the track, or the court feeling entirely ready for every element of the competition. Just as Michaels and his team take the stage at 11:30 pm, athletes take the plunge because it's game time. The lesson here is that waiting for perfect readiness can lead to missed opportunities, stagnant growth, and the paralysis of overthinking. Athletes should strive for the "excellent" zone, where they've put in the work, gained the knowledge, and developed the skills to perform at their best, even if the spotlight feels too bright. By understanding that perfection is more elusive than a mirage and that excellence is the true benchmark to aim for, athletes can embark on a journey of growth and achievement grounded in reality and marked by consistent progress.

Why don't we replace the age-old adage "Practice makes perfect" with "Practice makes excellent." Perfection remains an impossible target for athletes, as in many aspects of life, often leading to disappointment and frustration. Embracing excellence as the goal, on the other hand, allows athletes to push their boundaries and reach new heights. It's about being prepared, committed, and focused, ready to perform even when the pressure is on. By making this shift, you build a mindset that thrives on progress, learns from mistakes, and embraces challenges. So, remember, in pursuing your athletic endeavors, let excellence be your guiding star, and you'll find a path filled with growth, achievement, and the satisfaction of a job well done.

SWITCHING YOUR MINDSET

Transitioning from a fixed mindset to a performance-oriented one involves utilizing psychological tools mentioned previously but applied specifically to improve thinking. Here's a rundown of these tools with examples of how different athletes could employ each one with the assistance of their inner coach.

Journal prompt

Whilst reading through the following examples, consider how you might employ these strategies.

Mindfulness and self-awareness

Inner coach guidance: Your inner coach encourages you to observe your thoughts and reactions objectively, facilitating a shift from negative or limiting beliefs.

Alexis, a squash player struggling after consecutive losses, uses mindfulness techniques suggested by her inner coach. Alexis starts reframing these thoughts by acknowledging her frustrations and her self-doubts during practice. She gradually shifts her focus from fear of failure to learning from mistakes, enhancing her performance mindset.

Performance mindset cultivation

Inner coach guidance: Your inner coach emphasizes learning and growth, urging you to view setbacks as stepping stones for development.

Michael, a young swimmer, used to feel defeated after races where he didn't win. His inner coach encourages him to focus on improvement rather than just winning. Michael starts setting personal goals to beat his lap times, fostering a mindset of continual progress rather than fixed outcomes.

Positive self-talk

Inner coach guidance: Your inner coach emphasizes the importance of positive affirmations to counter self-doubt and limiting beliefs.

Track athlete Liz struggles with self-doubt before competitions. With her inner coach's guidance, she creates positive affirmations like "I am strong and capable" or "I have trained hard and am ready." This practice replaces her negative thoughts, boosting her confidence and race-day performance.

Goal setting

Inner coach guidance: Your inner coach supports you in setting specific, measurable, and challenging goals focused on sporting excellence.

Alex, an ice-hockey player, often felt stagnant in his skills. With his inner coach's guidance, he sets goals to improve his cross-ice passes and defensive strategies. As he consistently works towards these goals, Alex experiences growth in his abilities, leading to a more performance-driven approach.

Resilience building

Inner coach guidance: Your inner coach encourages you to embrace challenges as growth and character development opportunities.
A soccer player, Ethan encounters a period of injuries affecting his game. His inner coach helps him view this setback as a chance to improve his mental strength and focus on recovery exercises. Overcoming this challenging phase, Ethan emerges stronger and more resilient in his gameplay.

Visualization and mental rehearsal

Inner coach guidance: Your inner coach promotes visualization techniques to prepare for performances and build confidence mentally.
Maya, a gymnast, struggled with nerves during competitions. Her inner coach guides her through visualization exercises, imagining flawless routines and envisioning herself confidently executing each move. This mental rehearsal enhances her self-assurance and performance execution.

Embracing discomfort

Inner coach guidance: Your inner coach encourages you to step out of your comfort zone, embracing discomfort as a pathway to growth.
Daniel, a golfer, was apprehensive about trying new swing techniques. With the advice of his inner coach, he starts experimenting during practice rounds, tolerating initial discomfort. Over time, he adapts to the changes, significantly improving his accuracy and distance.

Seeking support and feedback
Inner coach guidance: Your inner coach motivates you to seek guidance and feedback for continuous improvement.
Maria, a long-distance runner, actively seeks feedback from her coach and peers on her pacing and technique. Embracing constructive criticism suggested by her inner coach, Maria adjusts her training regimen, improving performance and endurance.

When applied with an inner coach's guidance, these tools empower athletes to overcome fixed thinking and transition toward a more performance-oriented mindset, fostering growth, resilience, and enhanced performance in their respective sports.

This chapter delves into the challenges encountered in sports and outlines strategies to transition from a fixed mindset to a more adaptable, performance-oriented one. The lessons from the World Cup are a good example of how adverse situations can be used to build resilience and maintain the best mindset in preparation for performance.

KEY TAKEAWAYS AND INNER COACH GUIDANCE:

Embracing adversity with a Fortunately/Unfortunately mindset

Task: Practice the fortunately/unfortunately thinking strategy by applying it to everyday situations reframing negatives into positives.

Inner coach guidance: Encourage mental flexibility by swiftly reframing situations. Your inner coach can guide you in acknowledging that challenges present opportunities for growth and learning.

Striving for excellence over perfection

Task: Shift your focus from perfection to excellence. Set achievable goals and aim for progress instead of striving for an unattainable ideal.

Inner coach guidance: Your inner coach can emphasize excellence, fostering motivation and consistent improvement rather than fixating on flawlessness.

Utilizing psychological tools for flexible thinking

Task: Apply mindfulness, performance mindset, positive self-talk, goal setting, resilience building, visualization, embracing discomfort, and seeking support in your athletic journey.

Inner coach guidance: Leverage these tools with the help of your inner coach to transition from fixed thinking to a performance-oriented mindset. Your inner coach can provide support and guidance as you implement these strategies in your daily routine.

Journal Prompt: Things you can try

Mindfulness: Acknowledge self-doubts and reframe negative thoughts with the guidance of your inner coach.

Performance mindset: Set personal goals for continual progress, with an emphasis on learning and development.

Positive self-talk: Create affirmations to boost confidence, for constructive and helpful self-talk.

Goal setting: Focus on specific skill improvements for setting challenging yet achievable goals.

Resilience building: View setbacks as opportunities for growth, be grateful for the challenges.

Visualization: Mentally rehearse successful performances with the help of your inner coach's visualization techniques.

Embracing discomfort: Step out of your comfort zone to improve, guided by your inner coach's encouragement for growth through discomfort.

Seeking support: Actively seek feedback for continuous improvement, supported by your inner coach's emphasis on learning from others.

By applying these strategies and tools with the guidance of your inner coach, you can effectively adopt a more adaptable, growth-oriented mindset. This shift will help you to confront challenges confidently, foster resilience, and elevate your overall performance.

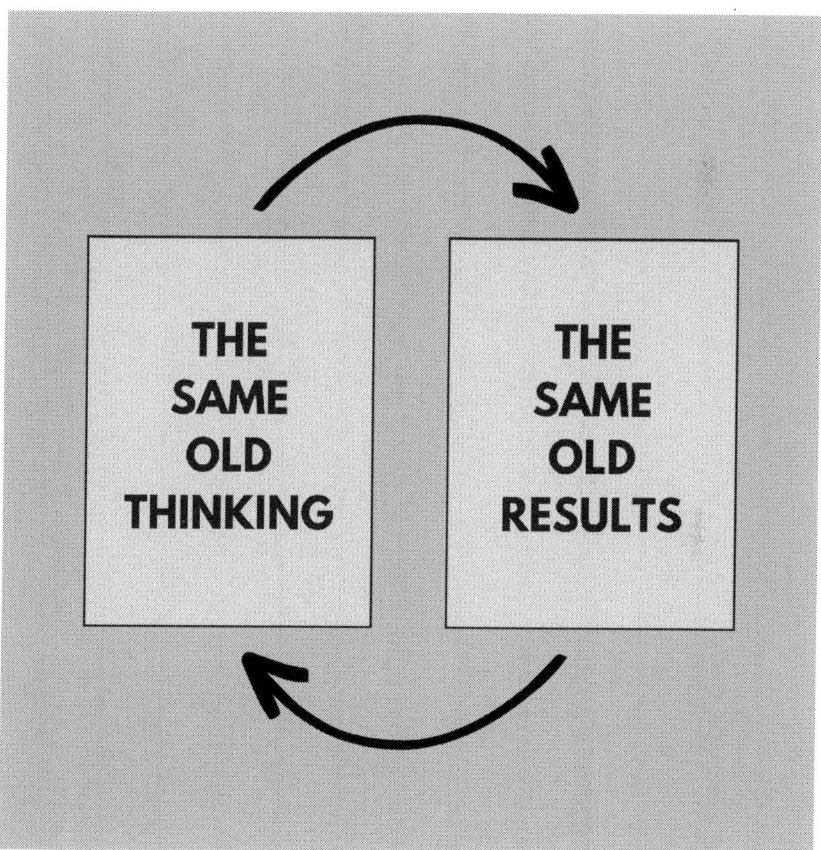

CHAPTER FIVE
CONQUER DOUBT AND NEGATIVITY

"The only limit to our realization of tomorrow will be our doubts of today."
Franklin D. Roosevelt

DON'T THINK ABOUT THE EIFFEL TOWER

At a local council pool, a lesson in success was on display at the pool deck. Beside the 25 m learn-to-swim pool, a safety message had been painted on the ground for children under 10 years. The message read, "Caution: No running."

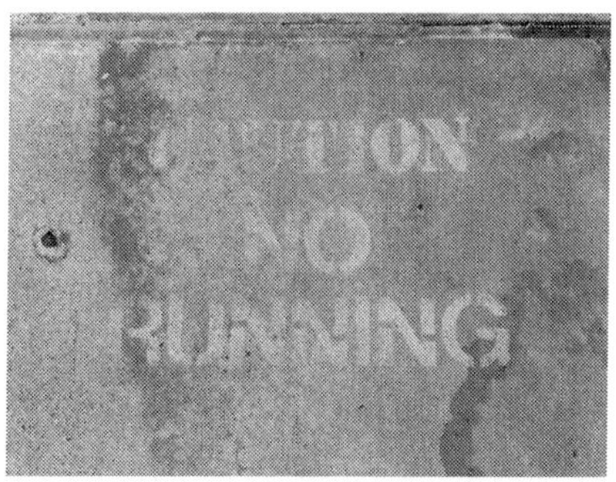

This message highlights the importance of focusing on success rather than avoiding failure. By emphasizing the action not to take, "no running," the children are directed towards a negative outcome. It also requires additional mental activity to decide upon the correct action. The problem with this instruction is it only tells you what to avoid. So, to get closer to the desired behavior, the reader must understand the instructions and then process the preferred action. This confusion could be avoided with a different message for the signage: WALK!

The signage on the pool deck reminds us that a positive, proactive message will be more effective in achieving our goals and reaching success, whether in sports or life. This warning is a great example of how to overly complicate a message. Rather than focus on the desired behavior, the messaging primes those who read it to lean towards the wrong behavior.

Create successful images in your mind through the language you use and how you speak to others.

Internally, the language you use in your thoughts directly impacts your mental imagery. By choosing affirmative and optimistic words when thinking about your goals, performance, and potential outcomes, you shape a mental landscape conducive to success. For instance, instead of dwelling on self-doubt or negative thoughts, consciously use phrases such as "When I do this," "I'm capable and prepared," or "I am continuing to improve." This positive self-talk enhances your mental imagery, creating mental pictures of success and reinforcing belief in your abilities.

Crafting successful mental images through the words of your inner coach requires deliberately choosing words that uplift and motivate you internally while projecting confidence and determination in your external interactions. Doing this will help you to shape a positive and helpful mindset, influencing your thoughts, actions, and eventual outcomes in your athletic pursuits.

Many years ago, I worked with a boxer. The presenting issue was that at the commencement of each round, he would quickly move from the center of the ring to his back on the ropes. It's certainly not a dominant place to position yourself in a fight. The questions I asked soon revealed that the parting word from his trainer as he stepped into the ring was, "Stay off the ropes." Humans are often visual in their processing of information. Therefore, when hearing the trainer's words, the fighter heard, "~~Stay off the~~ ropes." That was exactly where he ended up.

My advice? Change the phrasing. The intent of the message the trainer needed to give stayed the same; only the wording required needed to change. I asked the trainer the outcome he wanted, and he replied, "Stay in the center of the ring." The boxer's behavior instantly changed when the wording switched from "off the ropes" to "in the center."

The key takeaway lies in recognizing that during high-intensity moments, such as a boxing match or racing to reach the end of the pool first, the brain's processing capacity diminishes. In these situations, clear, direct, and focused instructions become paramount for achieving success for yourself and those around you.

Applying this principle in various aspects of life reveals its relevance. For instance, clear and concise instructions enhance the likelihood of favorable outcomes in competitive scenarios beyond sports—such as critical decision-making in a fast-paced work environment or navigating challenging personal situations. The principle extends to communication, leadership, and personal goal setting, emphasizing simplicity and directness to optimize performance and results. Understanding and implementing this approach can significantly impact success across different domains, underlining its versatility and broad applicability.

The applications of this principle in your life are limitless.

Instead of: Don't hit the snooze button. . .

Say: Get up when the alarm goes off

Instead of: . . . Don't eat junk food

Say: Choose a healthy food option

Instead of: . . . Don't leave a mess

Say: Tidy the kitchen

Instead of: . . . Don't be late

Say: Be on time

Instead of: . . . Don't sit on social media

Say: Read a book

Instead of: . . . Don't be shy

Say: Raise your hand and speak up

During the groundwork for this book, much consideration went into its title. Crafting a book title involves a deliberate, thoughtful process. Staying true to my guidance, I named this book *Belief*. I settled on this title as it communicates the book's commitment to its readers. If I had chosen a more pessimistic route, the book might have borne the title "Don't doubt yourself!" Both titles carry the same message but deliver them in completely different ways.

Whether it's poolside signage or a boxer's positioning in the ring, the power of language in shaping behavior is paramount. In both instances, the phrasing of instructions plays a significant role in directing actions. The overarching lesson from these stories is clear:

simplicity and directness in instructions are necessary during critical moments. Instructions emphasizing what to avoid, like "No running," often lead to confusion and unintended consequences. Instead, proactive, and positive directives, like "WALK," guide individuals more effectively toward the desired behavior.

These stories remind us of the importance of language in influencing our thoughts and actions. We can steer ourselves and others toward success by choosing affirmative and clear language. Whether in sports, decision-making, communication, or personal growth, the phrasing we use plays a fundamental role in leading us toward our goals.

MIND RACES: TAMING MENTAL OVERDRIVE

"Sometimes, I feel like my mind is in a race. I haven't finished one move, and I'm already mentally onto the next, or worse, I'm stuck in the past point. It's like my brain doesn't know how to hit the 'pause' button," Jamie lamented.

Jamie found herself at a crossroads as an elite badminton player with a promising career path. Her talent was undeniable, but the mental frustration of overthinking was holding her back from achieving her true potential.

"In badminton, split-second decisions matter. But when your mind is racing ahead, staying grounded in the present is hard. I knew I needed to find a way to quieten the noise in my head," Jamie admitted, reflecting on her struggles.

Amidst her training sessions and tournaments, Jamie grappled with an internal battle, recognizing that her success lay in mastering her mental game.

"I've been labeled an 'overthinker' since I first started playing, but I needed to understand what that truly meant for me. It's more than just thinking a lot; it's about how those thoughts disrupt my focus and sabotage my performance," Jamie acknowledged, determined to unravel the complexities of her thinking.

"I want to be fully present on the court, reacting instinctively to each point. I don't want my thoughts to overshadow my potential. It's about finding that mental switch to turn off the overthinking," she asserted, demonstrating her determination to conquer her mental hurdles and redefine her badminton career.

I have encountered countless athletes grappling with the label of being an "overthinker." What intrigues me most about this term is its frequency among athletes across various sports. It's often casually thrown around, yet it carries profound implications for an athlete's performance and mental state.

Delving into the depths of what it truly means to be an "overthinker" is where the journey toward regaining control commences. It's not simply about the volume of thoughts, but the disruptive impact on an athlete's focus, decision-making, and overall performance. Peeling back the layer of this label requires deciphering how these racing thoughts interfere with an athlete's ability to stay present, make split-second decisions, and perform at their peak.

Some people spend more time "inside their head" than others. Some people are highly analytical and critical, searching for meaning, considering every nook and cranny of how to be better. Other people are less so. Some cruise through, spending less time analyzing, and when they notice something, can move on without hanging on to the previous moment or agonizing over the next one.

When someone tells me they are an overthinker, I always ask them to consider what that label means. We are, of course, meant to be thinkers. Our brain provides us with many functions, and our commentary by our inner coach is an important part of keeping us alive and making good decisions. The "overthinker" will tell me that they are burdened with too much dialogue and thoughts that take over and distract their decision-making. This busyness of thinking has an emotional impact and will increase worry and anxiety. This was very much the case for Jamie; she said that the more she tried to take charge and direct her focus, the worse it got. Feeling like you are battling your brain is the first part of the puzzle to overcome. The driven, analytical, motivated athlete is probably not overthinking but more likely needs a strategy to quieten the chatter and create a clear path for performing without overwhelm.

SEVEN TRAPS OF EXCESSIVE MENTAL INVESTMENT

I have noticed many downsides for the athlete who defines themselves as an overthinker. The challenge with over-investing in our thinking is that it can create *illusions in our mind*, which we mistakenly believe to be *facts*. If we can accept the *truth*, we will be much better placed for success. Following is a description of the seven traps of excessive mental investment, illustrated through the experiences of athletes from different sports.

1. *Pursuit of perfection*
Illusion: Morgan, a dedicated diver, constantly feels the pressure to achieve absolute perfection in her routines, believing that any mistake renders her efforts futile.
Truth: Striving for perfection in diving is an unattainable goal (even though you can technically be awarded 10/10!). Morgan should instead focus on continuous improvement, setting achievable goals, and appreciating the hard work she invests in each training session. It's through this journey that true progress, and high performance is created.

2. *Low self-esteem*
Illusion: Nathan, an enthusiastic lacrosse player, frequently grapples with self-doubt, worrying that his performance on the field may not meet expectations or be appreciated by his team. This lack of confidence often inhibits his engagement and hinders his ability to fulfill his role on the team.
Truth: Like every lacrosse player, Nathan possesses unique talents and strengths. Strengthening his self-esteem involves acknowledging and embracing these qualities and understanding that the journey of

improvement is rewarding and valuable. Mistakes happen to all players, including his teammates; the key lies in how they are addressed and overcome.

3. *Fear of failure*
Illusion: Chloe, a determined surfer, views failure (errors) as a sign of incompetence, which makes her nervous about making mistakes during crucial competitions. She would rather not compete in some events than risk not performing to her high standards.
Truth: Errors are an inherent part of sport. Chloe must embrace mistakes as invaluable learning experiences that refine her surfing skills and foster her resilience and determination. Chloe would do well to treat mistakes as lessons getting her closer to success, rather than as moments of failure.

4. *Fear of rejection*
Illusion: James, an enthusiastic dodgeball player, constantly worries that any missteps or less-than-perfect performances will result in criticism and rejection from coaches, teammates, or fans.
Truth: Criticism is part of an athlete's life and doesn't define James's overall worth as a player. Constructive feedback can be a stepping stone to growth, and rejection can lead to even better learnings and opportunities. James should remain focused on his journey and not be disheartened by the opinions of others. Understanding the control element of his performance will assist him to improve in this area.

5. *Paralysis by analysis*
Illusion: Taylor, a dedicated triathlete, frequently experiences worry, especially under pressure. This creates fear of the consequence of wrong decisions and can paralyze her performance. Her words to describe those moments is, "I can actually feel myself *freeze up*."
Truth: In the world of triathlon, quick decision-making can be crucial, particularly in race tactics. Taylor should understand that no decision is infallible, to trust her training and instincts, make the best

choice in the moment, and adapt as circumstances evolve. A decision made is often better than an opportunity lost.

6. *Need for control*
Illusion: Chris, a committed rower, believes that meticulous control over every detail guarantees success, and he dreads unexpected challenges and changes to routine. If things don't go exactly as he wants/expects them to, he becomes anxious and upset.
Truth: Sports are inherently unpredictable, and Chris can't micromanage every racing aspect. He should embrace uncertainty and focus on what he can control—such as his preparation, mental attitude, and response to unforeseen circumstances. When challenges come along, he can welcome them as opportunities to build his cognitive flexibility.

7. *Mind in turmoil*
Illusion: Jessica, a determined racquetball player, believes that excessive worry and fear are justifiable and that predicting negative outcomes is necessary to prepare mentally. She describes her preoccupation with the worst case scenario as inevitable, even though it makes her feel physically unwell.
Truth: Anxiety can impede an athlete's performance by magnifying potential problems. Jessica needs a more balanced approach to managing what might go wrong versus what is going well. Jessica can learn to manage worry through relaxation techniques, mindfulness, and visualization. Staying present during training and competitions, concentrating on the process rather than worrying about outcomes, can enable her to perform at her best.

My partner is an expert in the business world. Therefore, plenty of financially based analogies are used in our household. So, to borrow from his world, thinking can be likened to financial investments. Investing is often a wise strategy as it builds our assets and gives us greater opportunities in the future. Our future economic success relies on our decisions about how much money we will put into a particular asset. Sometimes, we regret putting too much money into an investment; other times, we rue the missed opportunity by not investing more. So, too, there is a "sweet spot" for our thinking. Think too much about something, and you will spin around in mental circles, wasting time, not getting any closer to a decision, raising your blood pressure, and possibly losing valuable sleep. If you do not think about something enough, you'll be underprepared and may not make the best decision when required. Our thinking *investments* require us to not overspend nor underinvest.

SO, IF NOT OVERTHINKING, WHAT IS IT?

The first step of a successful strategy is recognizing that thinking and thinking (a lot) is normal for many people. The chatter within your head is your brain doing what it is supposed to do. If Jamie has a tournament starting tomorrow, her thinking drifts to traveling to the courts, her preparation, and thoughts about her opposing player. Then she notices she's just thought through many things happening tomorrow. She turns her attention to how much she thinks about what is happening. Then her inner coach tells her she probably does that more than other athletes, "Once again, here you are overthinking."

Calling yourself an "overthinker" is worsening the issue! So, if as you read this, you have ever referred to yourself as an overthinker, the first thing you can do is take that label off yourself! Your ability to think through what has happened, what is happening, and what might happen is a skill. It's an asset. What will benefit you is when you think in a way that is helpful, with the optimal amount of investment.

HOW, THEN, CAN WE DEFINE THIS FOR OURSELVES IN A BETTER WAY?

An alternative to defining yourself as an overthinker is to consider yourself a *thought strategist*. Embracing your ability to think deeply and analyze situations from various angles can be valuable, particularly in important decision-making scenarios. By recognizing your tendencies as a form of thorough deliberation, you can leverage this skill to make well-informed choices, solve intricate problems, and enhance your creativity. Having strategies to dial back the intensity and spin of unhelpful thoughts will help you not lie awake at 2 am, staring at the ceiling.

This book explores many thinking strategies to assist your inner coach. For some athletes, instead of clarity, some methods may unintentionally contribute to an already bustling mental landscape. Not every strategy in this book will work for every athlete. Sometimes, it is trial and error to work out (with your inner coach) what is best for you. I have had athletes over the years who don't respond to some of the cognitive strategies. Not every strategy works for every athlete. For some, it can feel like "thinking about the thinking" only adds to the problem. The good news is that there's another route to consider —using non-thinking strategies that benefit thinking.

When I began working with Jamie, I introduced her to a cognitive strategy involving a cue word (further detailed in Chapter 8), a proven effective method for many competitors. Yet, upon her return the following week, Jamie expressed a lukewarm response, "It was alright, I guess." Delving further, she clarified, "No, it wasn't okay—it simply didn't work. I must have done it wrong." Upon careful examination, it became apparent that Jamie had executed the strategy exactly as instructed. The issue wasn't her execution or the plan itself; rather, it was a matter of the strategy not aligning with Jamie's needs. Luckily, there is always another strategy to try!

I soon realized that, instead of responding to the cue word with immediate action, Jamie was caught up in an ongoing internal dialogue about what was happening, what wasn't happening, and why she shouldn't be feeling a certain way. For Jamie, the strategy triggered more self-talk, exacerbating the issue rather than alleviating it. Her inner coach was in overdrive, and she didn't feel she could stop it. A different approach was necessary to regain control because thinking about thinking (known as metacognition) was making the problem worse, not better. Essentially, we had two options: "thinking our way to success" or "behaving our way to success." It was time for Jamie to embrace the latter, allowing her actions to bring her the mental clarity she needed.

It might be time for a physical solution when your thought strategist goes into overdrive. Jamie needed to dial down her thought process, reduce the racing of her heart, and lower her blood pressure. She needed to play badminton without constantly engaging in a mental battle with herself. Her inner coach was making things worse. So, I turned to a strategy that could be applied anywhere, requiring no external resources or higher-level thinking, and could be discreetly utilized during competition without her opposing player or any spectator being aware of her actions. This technique, known as "anchoring," involves a two-part approach that combines a breathing strategy with a further physical action. Anchoring is a strategy to help regain focus and control. It's a strategy that calms down any scattered thinking, brings your focus back to the here and now, and calms your body so that it's ready to perform.

Part one–Breath control to harness your strength amidst action: Amidst the heat of competition, master your breath. Take a moment, grounded in your stance, eyes sharp or closed, and tune into each inhale and exhale. Feel the rhythm, the rise and fall of your chest or belly, syncing with your movements. You seize control by zeroing in on your breath, inviting a calm focus that fuels your body and mind. This deliberate act primes you for steadier, deeper breaths, calming your pulse and relaxing tense muscles. Elevate your performance through the power of controlled breathing.

Part two–Physical anchoring: Besides controlled breathing, physical anchoring can be a powerful technique to center yourself and take control of your thinking. Bring your thumb and first finger together with one hand, and then release them. Notice the sensation as your fingers touch and then part. As you continue, move on to your thumb and index finger, experiencing the connection and separation. Progress to your third finger, fourth, and finally, your little finger. With each repetition, you create a physical anchor that grounds you in the present moment.

This technique serves a dual purpose: it acts as a distraction from unhelpful thoughts while also serving as a reset practice for transitioning into the next phase of your competition. It redirects your attention towards the physical action, specifically focusing on your fingers. This intentional focus is a temporary diversion that slows down your thought process. Engaging in this technique provides a momentary pause, allowing you to regain composure and make more deliberate and thoughtful decisions moving forward.

The combination of regulated breathing and physical action is pivotal because both components exist in the present moment, the *now*. When you touch your fingertips, you are present in the here and now. This strategy can even be practiced while multitasking—for instance, holding this book with one hand while simultaneously applying the technique as you read this sentence. It's a means to draw yourself into the "now" and harness the control that this very moment offers.

Jamie was keen to try a new strategy, particularly when she realized it wasn't her fault the last one didn't work! Returning the next week, Jamie was much happier. The strategy had worked! She utilized it between every point, as she returned either to serve or to get into position to receive the serve from her opposition. I didn't think she would use it as often, but it worked well for her. She said she felt calmer, more in control, and exceeded the expectations set before the game.

Once you have a strategy to steady your breathing and calm your mind, you will likely be ready to understand how overthinking affects your life and the reality that might help you overcome it.

The great thing about the anchoring technique is that you can use it in many aspects of competition and training and as part of your every day. The more often you use it outside of competition, the more likely you will turn to it during competition. Here are some other situations where you could use the anchoring technique with controlled breathing:

- sitting at traffic lights, waiting for them to change
- when you are on hold on a phone call
- standing, waiting for the kettle to boil
- sitting in a meeting when a contentious issue is being discussed
- in a break in practice/training
- after making a mistake
- after doing something well

When could you use this anchoring technique? You might like to make some notes in your journal on how you can use this.

BELIEVE IT TO ACHIEVE IT: THE POWER OF SELF-EFFICACY

Within sports psychology, one fundamental truth reigns supreme: our thoughts become our reality. These thoughts inevitably materialize through our actions, forging lasting habits that dictate our triumphs and predict our setbacks. I repeat Henry Ford's famous words: "Whether you think you can or think you can't, you're right!"

In sports, this phrase is understood as *self-efficacy*. Self-efficacy reflects the self-belief of your ability. When your self-efficacy is high, you trust your capabilities in a specific task, such as executing a layup in basketball. Conversely, low self-efficacy might make you second-guess your competency, such as feeling uncertain about your tennis forehand. Self-efficacy is paramount as it can dictate your willingness to take on a task. You may readily embrace new challenges but shy away from tasks where previous struggles or low self-confidence prevail.

Consider the situation of Dave, a footballer whose role involved executing difficult high catches, a skill vital to the team's success. Yet, in a high-stakes match, he made a critical error, dropping the ball, resulting in the team conceding points and ultimately losing the game. In that pivotal moment, he transitioned from a capable player to one filled with self-doubt. He found himself reliving the moment in his mind over and over again. Each time, his inner coach became more critical and resolved his perception that he couldn't be trusted to catch a high ball. Despite a track record of success, that single mistake in a key moment profoundly shaped his self-perception, causing him to avoid being in the situation again.

Whether anchored in reality or not, self-efficacy profoundly influences your performance and overall success. The impact on confidence will be important when efficacy runs parallel to confidence. In the case of Dave, it was—his thoughts, beliefs about competence, and self-esteem were intrinsically tied to a single experience. When a skill he prided himself on faltered at a crucial moment, he didn't forgive himself for a human error under immense pressure. Instead, he labeled himself as useless, inadequate, and a failure. Even though he had years of evidence to say he could do it, that moment was significant enough for him that he not only questioned his ability to do that task but did not put himself in a position to do so for the following three years.

Regardless of how closely the reality of your ability and the perception of your ability are aligned, self-efficacy holds substantial influence over our performance and, ultimately, our success. It's a powerful force that fuels our determination and confidence and shapes our performance. Your belief in your abilities, regardless of any external factors, is the driving force that propels you to overcome challenges, achieve your goals, and conquer any obstacle.

In sports and life, self-efficacy is a silent but formidable ally. It instills an unshakable faith that you can triumph over adversity, even when the odds are stacked against you. This unwavering self-belief fuels your determination and empowers you to forge ahead relentlessly. Conversely, when your self-efficacy wavers and you doubt your capabilities, your performance can suffer significantly. These doubts cast a shadow over your potential, making you question your capacity to excel. They can even deter you from taking on challenges, decreasing your chances of success.

In essence, self-efficacy is the foundation upon which your achievements depend. Regardless of your natural talents, they can only be fully utilized if you have belief in what you can do. Your self-efficacy determines your readiness to confront training and competing head-on, and will influence your resolve to persevere no matter what. Belief in your abilities is a guiding compass, leading you toward victory, regardless of the obstacles or challenges.

Importantly, self-efficacy is only sometimes directly related to self-esteem. On a personal note, my tennis forehand is far from stellar. However, I have no aspirations of becoming a tennis pro, and my self-worth isn't contingent on my tennis skills. I accept my mediocre tennis abilities without them affecting my overall self-confidence.

As an athlete, you might find yourself in a situation where you are highly self-critical despite your potential and abilities. It's a challenge when you're fully aware of your capabilities yet allow your inner coach to be overly critical. Mental self-sabotage is a reality that can affect athletes of different sports, all ages, and levels of ability. I advise athletes to invest time in recognizing and acknowledging their strengths. Such reflections offer a counterbalance to the mistruths of being too critical. Due to a common human response called *the negativity bias,* we often dwell more on our shortcomings, giving them undue weight in our thinking. However, to maintain sustained success, you must also consider what you do well. Focusing solely on shortcomings and defeats won't allow you to reproduce the components that lead to success.

One practical strategy is to keep a *high-five* diary. A record of the small and large successes to keep your mindset positively focused. You don't need an entire training session or competition to be outstanding; the key is to celebrate the small victories. Record these moments in a notebook, along with the date and event, like this:

Monday, July 6th – Gym session
I executed the core session well and maintained excellent form during the bench press.

By acknowledging your successes, you create a tangible record of your achievements. While it may not instantly instill self-belief, it serves as evidence of the elements you do well. This practice shifts your focus from negativity to positivity, a valuable step for enhancing performance. The physical record is important and can be a helpful resource to look back upon the small wins, at times when you need them.

Ultimately, belief must come from within. Confidence can't be handed to you, but you can create an environment where it's okay to consider your accomplishments with humility. I clarify to athletes that success revolves around understanding and recognizing what they excel at. Focusing on your accomplishments reinforces the successful actions you need to repeat through your competitions.

As an athlete, you act as your own trusted advisor in these discussions. Stay open to evaluating your strengths, limitations, efforts, and accomplishments. This will help you understand and improve your self-belief and capabilities, influenced by your inner coach.

WHY IMPOSTER SYNDROME DOESN'T EXIST

Jackson, an accomplished basketball coach who ascended through division competitions, reached a new pinnacle when he was appointed as head coach of the Raptors. Outwardly, he exuded confidence: possessing a remarkable basketball IQ, was highly respected by his players, and boasted an impressive win/loss record. Yet, inwardly, a different narrative unfolded. Despite his assured exterior, Jackson grappled with moments of self-doubt. He questioned his abilities, wrestling with doubts about his competence and fearing imminent exposure of his suitability as a college coach. Adding to his turmoil, he noticed a disturbing sensation while courtside—his legs quivered, teetering on the brink of giving way. Amidst these doubts, he felt the weight of responsibility—he realized countless people depended on him. He couldn't shake the feeling that he somehow fluked into this position, and the thought of letting everyone down was unbearable. He often pondered how he could sustain success in a role that seemed perpetually on the verge of collapse.

Have you ever reached significant milestones or received accolades only to feel your success was undeserved? That lingering sense that your accomplishments were merely strokes of luck rather than a result of your ability or hard work? This pervasive self-doubt, often called *imposter syndrome*, is more commonly experienced than most athletes and coaches realize. It's marked by an inner belief of being a fraud despite outward evidence pointing towards competence and success. Individuals grappling with imposter syndrome often find themselves in an internal struggle between their achievements and the persistent fear of being revealed as inferior. This mindset and the constant worry of others uncovering their shortcomings can lead to overwhelming stress and reluctance to pursue new opportunities or fully embrace one's capabilities. In this scenario, the inner coach is always on the job raising self-doubt, and tearing down your confidence if you don't get a handle on it.

But what if I told you there's a way to break free from the grip of imposter syndrome? What if there's a strategy to manage the doubt rather than allowing it to control you? Let's start with the facts. In psychology, there exists a comprehensive manual detailing psychological conditions and their diagnostic criteria. However, amid anxiety disorders, mood disorders, and other forms of human distress described in this extensive book (not exactly light reading material), there's an essential insight—a missing entry. Imposter syndrome isn't listed. It's not a recognized psychological condition. The reason you don't have it? Because no one does! I shared this revelation with Jackson, to which he responded, "Okay, Doc, but what does that mean? Because it feels undeniably real when I'm standing courtside." Here lies an important distinction—the symptoms are undoubtedly real, whether worry, sweating, shaking, wobbling in your shoes, or feeling sick. However, the syndrome itself isn't real.

Perceiving imposter syndrome as a syndrome can leave athletes with a sense of helplessness and belief of something beyond their control. Jackson was correct when he said how real the physical symptoms were, it's the conclusion that he was suffering from a syndrome that was both untrue and unhelpful. Let's help our inner coach to understand it better and free us from a syndrome that doesn't exist. Let's change our understanding from imposter syndrome to imposter thinking. Imposter thinking is the normal thoughts of self-doubt and insecurity experienced by athletes, even when evidence points to their competence and accomplishments. It's a common part of being human, prevalent among athletes, and not a specific diagnosable syndrome.

Acknowledging that occasional self-doubt and insecurity are normal experiences everyone shares is crucial. In sports, imposter thinking is part of the human journey and can be effectively managed and overcome with the right support and strategies. Recognizing imposter thinking empowers athletes by emphasizing that these thoughts are transient and feelings aren't permanent and can be altered.

Athletes can bolster their confidence and unlock their full potential on and off the field by taking charge of their thoughts and emotions. Training your inner coach to notice the moments of imposter thinking, and using some of the thinking strategies included within *Belief* and *Compete* will put you back in control of managing the wobbly moments. If you feel you need further assistance, collaborating with a mental health professional, being kind to yourself, and cultivating self-compassion are further effective ways to tackle imposter thinking. Seeking support from friends, family, or teammates can also be instrumental in navigating these challenges and fostering overall well-being.

Journal prompt

What are your thoughts about imposter thinking, and what is most helpful for you as an athlete when you notice moments of doubt?

Ctrl + Alt + Delete

Control your actions

Alter your perspective

Delete self doubt

CHAPTER SIX
NAVIGATING THE ROLLER COASTER OF EXPECTATIONS

"You always pass failure on your way to success."
Mickey Rooney

Meet Owen, a dedicated high school track athlete with an unwavering determination to qualify for the regional championship. He poured his heart and soul into rigorous training sessions, striving relentlessly toward his goal. However, his aspirations encountered an unexpected hurdle on the qualifying race day when an unforeseen injury during the heat disrupted his performance. Falling short of the qualifying time left Owen with feelings of disappointment and frustration. As a highly competitive athlete driven by success, he found it challenging to grapple with this setback, seeing it as a personal failure. Owen's emotional journey through disappointment begins here, setting the stage for his growth in handling setbacks as a young athlete.

Navigating disappointment can be tough, especially for athletes fueled by ambition and a drive to succeed. Setting a path to greatness can make the reality of small and large misfortunes feel frustrating, shocking, and, at times, completely unfair. It's crucial to realize that disappointment is a normal part of sport. It is on the road to success that disappointments can actually be helpful when experienced along the way. While it can feel little comfort to someone like Owen, who had his heart set on the championship, it can spur growth and improvement, possibly leading to greater success in the future.

Owen did not take the injury well. He fluctuated between stages of disbelief (telling his coach it wasn't so bad and he would be ready to train soon), frustration (snappy, and family found him difficult to be around), and wanting to do more recovery work against his trainer's caution. All these reactions are understandable and common grief stages in response to injury. However, they were not helping Owen, and he was feeling miserable—a classic case of pushing through a disappointment faster than is warranted. When we aim to "get over" disappointment quickly, we try to push away or ignore our feelings. We gloss over what we are feeling, and rather than disappear, those emotions sit in the background and bother us in a way we can't always see. Ultimately, this approach often leads to more stress and negative emotions. Disappointment is a complex emotion that can't simply be brushed aside.

Instead of rushing to "get over" disappointment, consider "traveling through" it. This means recognizing that disappointment is a natural human emotion. We all face it at different points, and it can serve as a powerful motivator for personal growth.

By "traveling through" disappointment, we acknowledge and work through our feelings constructively. This involves accepting our emotions, letting ourselves experience them fully, and using them as a catalyst for growth and development. Accepting an emotion can be a bitter pill to swallow. Acceptance means acknowledging the events and living with the feeling. The truth is that most people would rather not. Owen would rather push past the painful reality of missing the qualification and the setback of his progress by the injury. Facing it, accepting it, in a word, hurts.

In this process, we supercharge our emotional intelligence, resilience, and capacity to tackle future setbacks head-on. Rather than sweeping disappointment under the rug, mastering its management becomes a turbo-boost for personal growth and goal-crushing success. It's not just about enduring setbacks; it's about using them as rocket fuel for personal evolution. Embracing these emotions gives us an edge that sharpens our responses, fortifies our mindset, and amplifies our ability to conquer challenges. This isn't just about growth; it's about dominating with unmatched self-awareness and supreme emotional control, paving the way to alpha-level success in every facet of our lives.

Ignoring our feelings or pretending that upsetting situations didn't happen might seem like a temporary fix. However, it's like kicking a can down the road—eventually, it'll appear to trip us up. A seasoned coach once shared a valuable perspective with me: seeing an athlete's error as evidence of their effort. While repeated errors might not be as forgivable, learning happens beyond our comfort zones. Mistakes aren't the opposite of success; they're a part of the journey. A wise athlete understands the importance of failing fast and having effective strategies for recovering from mistakes. Error recovery involves acknowledging, understanding, and rectifying mistakes, leading to growth and improvement.

Owen's disappointment lingered, prompting his coach to encourage a different approach. Rather than hastily dismissing his feelings, Owen chose to confront his emotions head-on. Guided by his coach's advice, he began to see this setback not merely as a stumbling block but as an opportunity for growth and development. Owen acknowledged the inherent value of embracing disappointment as a part of his journey towards success. He understood that the path to achievement was not solely defined by victory but by the lessons learned through adversity.

I've used a helpful phrase when faced with challenging situations: "While I might not like it, I need to accept it." It's about giving yourself the space to acknowledge disappointment while recognizing that accepting what happened is crucial to moving ahead. Picture it as being stuck in a tough spot. Refusing to accept it is like staying trapped, but when you acknowledge it, it's like unlocking the door to finding a way out. It's not about pretending everything's fine; it's more about saying, "Okay, this happened. What's my next move to overcome it?" Accepting disappointments sets you free to rebound and come back stronger.

Driven by this newfound perspective, Owen focused on comprehending the circumstances of his injury. He adopted a proactive stance, recognizing that his setback could lead to improvement. With his coach's guidance, Owen delved deeper into understanding his limitations and devised strategies to prevent similar setbacks in the future. He embraced the idea that errors and setbacks were not indications of failure but stepping stones toward progress.

Owen cultivated resilience and a heightened ability to manage disappointments through his commitment to this approach. He learned that navigating through disappointment, rather than hastily trying to overcome it, allowed him to emerge stronger and more emotionally intelligent. Owen's journey exemplified the significant impact of embracing setbacks as opportunities for improvement, leading him to evolve as an athlete and an individual.

When confronted with disappointment next time, embrace "traveling through" rather than hastily trying to "get over" it. Though it might require time and effort, the outcome will be a stronger, more resilient, and emotionally adept version of yourself.

MASTERING EMOTIONAL TERRAIN: NAVIGATE AND DOMINATE

Disappointment and frustration are common reactions in sports when things are unplanned. These emotions, triggered by setbacks like missing a qualification time or coping with an injury, significantly impact mood and confidence. Acknowledging these feelings is essential as they represent the situation's significance. Your inner dialogue, often critical after such events, needs constructive engagement. Understanding and redirecting this inner coach's evaluation positively allows for emotional alignment with your goals.

Consider the case of Whitney, a dedicated track athlete. Despite her consistent training, she failed to qualify for a prestigious competition, leaving her immensely disappointed. Instead of brushing off her emotions, Whitney acknowledged her frustration and disappointment. She recognized that these feelings stemmed from the event's importance and her strong desire to compete. Whitney then consciously redirected her inner dialogue, shifting her self-critical thoughts into ways on how she could learn and improve for future races. Whitney's inner coach recognized, "This feels so unfair and upsetting (acknowledged). It makes sense because that competition meant so much, and I worked so hard to qualify, only to miss out (significance/importance). As disappointing as this is, it's okay that I'm upset. All I can do now is learn from the race and work on my start, which is where I can improve further (learn and improve)."

Personal-care revolution: Elevate your priority list

Maintaining physical health and a positive mindset amidst disappointment is crucial. It's easy to fall into negative habits like irregular sleep, unhealthy eating, or neglecting recovery. Focus on adequate rest, a nutritious diet, and regular physical activity. Additionally, include enjoyable activities, like spending time with friends, enjoying music, or reading.

Take inspiration from Austin, an ultimate frisbee player disappointed after losing a critical game. Instead of letting frustration take over, Austin focused on looking after himself. He ensured he rested sufficiently, maintained his healthy diet, and engaged in light workouts to recover in the days after the game. Alongside physical care, Austin spent time with friends, enjoying their company and using it as a source of positivity amidst the disappointment. Too often, athletes use the disappointment of a poor performance to punish themselves. By looking after himself, Austin focused on what he could control and what would set him up best for his next competition.

Strengthen your journey: Embrace support

Turning to teammates, coaches, or friends during tough times can provide valuable encouragement, advice, or a listening ear. Consider professional help from a therapist or counselor for comprehensive support during significant disappointments.

Reflect on the experience of Tyler, a swimmer who felt disheartened after missing a chance to run in the 4x100m relay team for his country at the World Championships. Tyler turned to his partner for support. By taking the time to share his disappointment, Tyler felt more supported, and talking aloud helped him gain some perspective. Whilst still disappointed, felt better for the conversation. Having someone to talk to gave Tyler emotional strength and reassurance during a challenging time.

Thriving mindset: Embrace growth potential

Reframe disappointment as an opportunity for learning and growth. Instead of self-criticism, adopt curiosity-driven questions to understand why things happened as they did. Emphasize the positive aspects of the situation, focusing on lessons learned and skills gained.

A cheerleader, Harper, encountered a setback when she and her team made some small errors and lost a competition to their main rival. Instead of dwelling on her mistakes, Harper embraced a performance mindset. She approached the situation with curiosity, asking herself what lessons could be learned. Harper focused on the positives of the performance, acknowledging her team's effort and identifying skills for improvement. This perspective shift enabled her to view the disappointment as a stepping stone for personal and team improvement.

Goalcraft: Forging fresh paths to success

Utilize disappointment as motivation to set new objectives and concentrate on progress. Identify specific skills for improvement and devise a plan to achieve these goals. This approach not only maintains focus but also enhances confidence for future endeavors.

Take a cue from Marcus, a water polo player who faced disappointment after receiving limited playing time despite his significant efforts in practice. Instead of dwelling on the limited time, Marcus channeled his disappointment into setting new goals. He identified areas of his defensive positioning as an area that required further improvement. He spent time with the defensive coach to learn new strategies to work on as additional practice sessions. This renewed focus motivated Marcus and boosted his confidence as he prepared for future competitions.

UTILIZING THE INNER COACH: MENTAL SUCCESS THROUGH NON-SELECTION

For a more in-depth case study, consider these strategies through Matai, who wasn't selected to play in the opening game for the softball season.

Matai is a talented player who worked hard through the tryout period for his new team. He felt confident in his skills and was excited about the opportunity to play in the opening game. Unfortunately, he received the news that he wasn't selected for the team. The feedback was that he had trialed well, but despite his capabilities, other athletes he was competing with were physically stronger and trialed better than he did. Given that he didn't do anything wrong, he's struggling with the disappointment and feeling somewhat hopeless about his circumstances. How might the strategies for disappointment help him in this situation?

Step one – Acknowledge and embrace your feelings:

When Matai recalled his self-talk since discovering the news, he knew that much of what he thought was unhelpful. He thought things to himself such as:

- "I'm not good enough; I'll never be good enough for them."

- "I must have messed up somewhere; it's all my fault."

- "They never appreciate my hard work; they don't value me as a player."

As a fierce competitor, Matai can fine-tune his mental approach with his inner coach, reshaping his words to be honest with himself and encourage himself moving forward. Instead of letting thoughts of falling short linger, he can reframe them to align with his competitive drive. When feelings of not meeting expectations arise, Matai could recognize them as valid without letting them define his worth as a player. Instead of blaming himself for failing, he can practice kindness by understanding that setbacks are part of the game and not every disappointment is solely his doing. Shifting from any sense of being undervalued, Matai can concentrate on personal improvement, seeing it as an opportunity to elevate his skills, regardless of external judgments. By embracing this mindset, Matai acknowledges his feelings and confronts and redirects his inner coach to fuel his resilience, turning setbacks into opportunities for greater success on the field.

Step two – Practice personal-care: Matai, as a driven and competitive athlete, places personal-care at the forefront, especially during intense times. He understands that both physical and emotional well-being are crucial. Ensuring he gets ample rest, recognizing that quality sleep fuels his top performance and mental clarity remains a non-negotiable aspect. Prioritizing nutritious meals and staying hydrated are fundamental; they provide the energy necessary to tackle the day's challenges head-on.

Personal-care isn't just about the physical; Matai gets that. For him, it's also about emotional strength. Hitting the gym isn't just a workout—it's a release, a way to channel any pent-up energy or stress. Beyond that, he carves out time for hobbies and moments with family and friends that recharge him. This rounded approach to personal-care fuels Matai, enabling him to face challenges with greater resilience.

Step three – Seek support: In his pursuit of excellence, Matai recognizes the power of seeking support, a trait of true strength. After facing disappointment, he opens up to his teammates and coach, not seeing it as a sign of weakness but a sign of his determination to bounce back stronger. Their words of encouragement and unwavering support became fuel for his resolve.

Matai doesn't stop there. He turns to his inner circle, confiding in his parents and closest friends. Their strong belief in him, their reassuring words, and the comfort of their support lifts his spirits during this challenging phase.

For Matai, seeking support isn't about dependency on others; it's a strategic move, a tool in his arsenal to reinforce his mental fortitude. It's a testament to his understanding that the path to success isn't a solitary journey but a team effort, drawing strength from those who believe in his potential. By embracing this support network, Matai not only rebuilds his resilience but also feels better supported and less isolated in a challenging time.

Step four – Reframe your perspective: Matai sees a chance to improve and strengthen despite the disappointment. He views this setback as an important lesson, a step towards enhancing his skills and knowledge. Instead of dwelling on the non-selection, he shifts his energy into analyzing the experience, separating the controllable from the uncontrollable, and working on his patience for future opportunities.

Matai's mindset shifts him to focus on the silver linings within the situation. Rather than fixating on the letdown, he zeroes in on the skills honed during the tryout process. He uses this as momentum, using these acquired skills to build towards improving as an athlete and refining his competitive edge. For Matai, setbacks aren't roadblocks but fuel for improvement, driving him closer to team selection.

Step five – Set new goals: Matai uses this disappointment as a motivator to set new goals and focus on moving forward. He identifies specific skills he wants to improve, such as base running and improving his fastball, and creates a plan to achieve those goals. He shifts his goal from making the team to improving his skills and making it impossible for the coach to not select him next time!

Matai's intelligent use of these strategies helps him navigate disappointment effectively. Though moving beyond this setback may take time, he knows patience, persistence, and a solid support system are vital.

This experience isn't solely about overcoming a setback; it's a chance for Matai to grow even stronger and more resilient. By adopting these strategies and staying committed, he's building the resilience to face future challenges. This process showcases how setbacks can be pivotal, highlighting the value of a helpful mindset paired with determination and persistence.

So, how much do you need to immerse yourself in errors and mistakes to uncover their valuable lessons? Finding the right balance between acknowledging mistakes and fixating on them is key for personal improvement.

After a competition, identifying missteps or overlooked opportunities is crucial for learning and improvement. However, the true skill lies not in fixating on the mistakes themselves but in mastering the art of error recovery. It's about paying enough attention to glean insights without lingering excessively on these errors. Effectively navigating this balance enables individuals to use these moments as catalysts for growth, focusing on constructive approaches rather than letting mistakes hinder future progress.

TURNING ERRORS INTO OPPORTUNITIES: USING REFLECTION, SHARING AND LEARNING

Sydney is a freshman collegiate racquetball player. In her debut game, she missed several key shots, leaving her frustrated and disheartened. Throughout the night, Sydney replayed those missed opportunities in her mind, unable to shake off the disappointment. Even during the following week's practices, the memories of her errors lingered, dampening her confidence and mood.

Sydney's intense focus on her mistakes prevented her from considering potential solutions. Dwelling on errors often leads to a decline in confidence, which can affect performance in future matches.

A better approach for Sydney is to view mistakes as learning opportunities. While she acknowledges her mistakes, her focus shifts to rectifying them for improvement. She may still be upset about the missed scoring opportunities, but her priority is to address those mistakes before the next game.

For instance, when Sydney reflects on her performance, she may analyze the potential causes of her missed shots. Was she too focused on the opposition? Did nervousness take over and affect her accuracy? After identifying the issue, Sydney can formulate a plan to enhance her focus, reaction time, or shot angles.

You can boost your confidence by extracting and applying feedback from a game or competition. Learning from mistakes necessitates self-reflection. You can gather feedback by posing questions such as:

- What was the situation?
- What went awry?
- What have I learned?
- What adjustments can I make?
- How will I work towards improving in this area?

Adhering to a specific process for addressing mistakes after each competition emphasizes improvement, safeguards your confidence, and mitigates the emotional toll of errors.

To aid athletes in their pursuit of improvement, I champion an approach centered on three pivotal elements: reflection, sharing, and learning. This methodology is an effective tool for athletes due to its inherent capacity to facilitate personal development and team enhancement.

Reflection is vital for athletes as it helps them break down their performances, spot areas to improve, and fine-tune their strategies. When teams promote open sharing among members, it builds a collaborative environment that brings diverse viewpoints together and fuels a shared ambition for success. Moreover, focusing on learning fosters a growth-oriented mindset, enabling constant progress by learning from successes and setbacks. This approach isn't only a step-by-step plan; it's a mindset aimed at helping athletes improve. It's flexible and works well within teams, making it a valuable tool for enhancing individual skills and creating a culture where everyone grows together.

The successful debrief

Kickoff: Begin by outlining the purpose of the debrief. Establish ground rules that underscore respect, confidentiality, and active listening in a team context. When engaging in self-reflection, remember why you're debriefing and the significance of approaching the debrief with kindness, curiosity, and honesty.

Replay the day: Describe the events under consideration without diving into analysis or interpretation. The goal is to establish a clear and shared understanding of what transpired, especially in a team context.

Emotional unpack: Acknowledge and validate the emotional responses the events elicit. Recognize and respect the feelings that emerge.

Decoding decisions: Delve into the decisions and actions taken during the event. Focus on understanding the reasons behind these decisions rather than dwelling on whether they were right or wrong. Encourage a constructive and collaborative discussion, especially within a team.

Lessons uncovered: Identify the key lessons gleaned from the experience and how they can inform future actions. Discuss future strategies for handling similar situations based on the insights gained.

Summing up: Summarize the key points and future actions identified during the debrief. Ensure there's a plan for follow-up and implementation in the future.

The personal voyage: Reflect on the discussion and identify your takeaways. Consider how the lessons learned can be applied to your journey.

Would you like a downloadable copy of the steps? If so, click on this QR code, and a copy will be sent to your inbox.

Elite athletes aren't flawless; they excel by converting mistakes into learning opportunities, with an inner coach guiding this new learning. Adopting a solution-driven approach is crucial to enhance performance. Setting up a post-competition feedback system helps you see what you did without bias, so you can develop a plan be better next time.

True resilience in athletes lies in seeing setbacks as chances for growth, not as insurmountable hurdles. Athletes like Matai and Sydney demonstrate this resilient mindset by leveraging their inner coaches, rethinking their approach, and setting new goals despite disappointment.

Prioritizing error recovery instead of fearing failure is key.

Journal prompt

How could you apply the debrief guidelines to assess your own performance? The debrief format is as effective for analyzing the performance of an individual as it is for a team.

Disappointments, failures, errors—however you wish to think about them, are all part of sport. It's what you do with those thoughts that becomes important. Acknowledging mistakes without fixating on them allows athletes to learn, improving their skills and resilience both on and off the field. The quicker you can recover from an error, the less mental energy you waste and can get back into performing.

For athletes on a similar path, self-reflection, getting support, changing perspectives, and setting new goals are key. Seeing setbacks as chances to grow builds a mindset focused on progress. Following these steps, guided by your inner coach, helps you become tougher, more flexible, and more successful, in both sports and life.

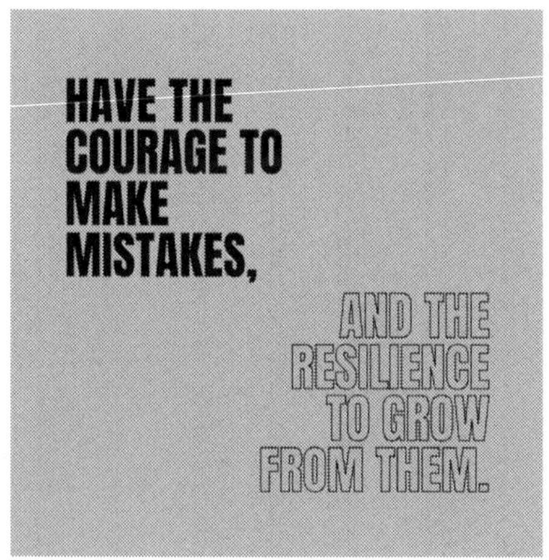

CHAPTER SEVEN
STRATEGIES FOR MENTAL OBSTACLES

"Doubt is only removed by action. If you're not working, then that's where doubt comes in."
Conor McGregor

LET'S consider the case of Ashton, a competitive cross-country runner striving to excel. Despite several victories and an impressive record, Ashton tends to fixate on his losses more than his wins. He has won numerous races but dwells on the races he lost, especially those where he has made tactical errors.

Ashton raced against a highly skilled runner who had traveled from another region to race him. Despite running exceptionally well after a poor start, he lost in a close finish. Although the run highlighted his strengths and effort, Ashton couldn't shake off the disappointment. He kept replaying the critical points in the race and thinking about what he could have done differently. Instead of focusing on the positives of the skills displayed in the race, he became consumed by the feeling of defeat.

After this result, Ashton's training sessions centered around his start. His thoughts often drifted back to the race, interfering with his focus during training sessions when he should have been fully immersed in the workout. Each time, his inner coach told him how foolish the start was, and he felt a strong sense of embarrassment and regret, wishing he could go back and run the race again.

He repeatedly practiced running at start pace when at practice, neglecting other aspects of his running that needed attention. With each mistake made during training, frustration would mount, weighing heavily on his confidence. Despite his coach's efforts to reassure and motivate him, Ashton's fixation on past losses only heightened the pressure and stress he felt leading up to future races.

Ashton's case exemplifies the negativity bias in athletes. Despite a series of victories and successful races, he fixates on his losses, allowing them to overshadow his achievements. His tendency to overthink defeat impacts his mindset, practice routines, and overall approach to the sport, affecting his performance and potentially his future races. Where you direct your attention is a fine balance. You want to focus enough on the areas for improvement without focusing "too much." It's a Goldilocks approach! Focusing too much on what went wrong causes you to get caught up in your thinking. You need more clarity to make wise decisions. Understanding and addressing this negativity bias will be crucial for Ashton to maintain a balanced perspective, learn from setbacks, and continue evolving as an athlete.

WINNING AGAINST THE NEGATIVITY ODDS: HOW YOU CAN FLIP THE SCORE

Competitive sport is filled with many mental challenges that can significantly influence the outcome you achieve and your overall well-being. The negativity bias is a mental bump that can profoundly affect athletes, coaches, and officials. It causes a stronger focus on negative experiences, setbacks, or criticism than achievements. It is a way of thinking that amplifies the bad and underestimates the good. Think of it like a filter that emphasizes the problems and minimizes the success. If your inner coach doesn't notice it happening, it can impact your mindset, emotions, and decision-making. In sports, the negativity bias can greatly affect your confidence, resilience, and overall performance.

Thanks to the negativity bias, it is not uncommon for athletes to fixate more on their mistakes and setbacks than on celebrating their successes. It makes sense when errors can be the difference between winning and losing—homing in on what goes wrong understandably grabs our attention. Focusing too much on mistakes can lead to overthinking, which then chips away at confidence and hurts future performance. Even with plenty of praise, negative comments hit hard, messing with an athlete's head and self-confidence.

When there exists an anticipation of making mistakes or failing, stress and pressure builds, causing increased worry and anxiety in crucial moments. The looming fear of failure creates a relentless pressure cooker for athletes, elevating stress levels unnecessarily. This fixation magnifies self-doubt, overshadows achievements, and sends morale and confidence on a downward spiral.

The negativity bias also influences memory retention, with athletes remembering and dwelling on past failures. This deep imprint in the memory banks can result in vividly replaying negative experiences. This hyper-focus on setbacks obstructs the assimilation of learning, hindering the ability to improve.

The anticipation of negative outcomes can paralyze an athlete's decision-making process. This can result in an athlete opting to avoid risks or challenges due to a fear of the consequences. Success in sports is often about an athlete's willingness to take calculated risks for success. A fear of failure and anticipating the worst can rob you of the courage to take a necessary risk.

It can be challenging to feel the weight of negativity and self-doubt. When it is ongoing, it can lead to feelings of exhaustion, reduced motivation, and sport can start to lose its enjoyment factor. A relentless presence of negativity tends to corrode self-esteem, increase doubt and reduce confidence in abilities. Understandably, maintaining a sense of self-assurance becomes increasingly challenging amidst this persistent negativity. Fortunately, there are strategies that can assist with this.

Managing the negativity bias is a key part of your psychology. It requires an ability to use strategies to counterbalance negative thoughts with positive ones, and learn from setbacks rather than dwell on them. Techniques like mindfulness, mental reframing, and negative thought conversion are useful. When you have a personal plan to counteract the negativity bias, both your performance and your well-being will benefit.

This cognitive tendency also impacts decision-making abilities and memory retention. Consequently, an athlete's overall well-being and self-esteem can significantly decline. Hence, what strategies are most effective in effectively handling the negativity bias within sports?

Mental reframing and gratitude: In the competitive realm, mental reframing and gratitude are great tools for navigating the highs and lows of sport. When faced with defeat or setbacks, being able to reframe these experiences as potential for improvement and learning will give you a significant mental edge. For example, a loss in a game can be viewed as a chance to analyze weaknesses and strategize for improvement rather than solely focusing on the loss. Acknowledging your physical prowess, the backing you receive, and the opportunity to pursue your passion in sports can cultivate a deep sense of gratitude. This appreciation fuels determination, propelling you to bounce back with even more strength. Such a positive outlook shields against demotivation and fosters a mindset centered on progress and advancement.

Mindfulness and awareness: Mindfulness is a game-changer for sharpening your mental game. When you're fully aware, you stay locked in during those make-or-break moments in competition. By practicing mindfulness techniques like focused breathing or visualization, you dial down the stress, amp up your concentration, and control your emotions. This mental toughness? It's what lets you stay cool under pressure, making those split-second decisions with laser-like precision. Using mindfulness not only enhances your focus but also enables you to swiftly recognize and dismiss negative thoughts or distractions, ensuring you remain laser-focused on dominating the field or court.

Challenge and replace negative thoughts: Challenging and replacing negative thoughts is an important skill for your performance. Recognizing exaggerated negative thinking patterns is the starting point to confront these thoughts head-on. By evaluating the validity of these thoughts and replacing them with more rational and positive ones, you can reduce negative thinking and its impact. For instance, instead of fixating on potential failure, you can redirect your focus to past achievements, or the progress made in training:

"I'm feeling really nervous about the upcoming race. What if I don't perform well and disappoint my team?"

"Wait a minute. Remember that race last season where I had that amazing comeback and crossed the finish line first? And what about earlier this year when I set a new personal record?"

"I've had some really strong performances in the past. I need to focus on those instead of worrying about what might go wrong. I've trained hard, and I know I have the ability to perform. I just need to trust in my training, execute my race plan and believe in myself."

This communication by your inner coach equips you with the mental strength to tackle challenges head-on even when under pressure.

DEFUSION FROM OUR THOUGHTS

In Ashton's journey, we witnessed the powerful grip of negativity bias on an athlete's mindset and performance. Despite a string of victories, his focus on past losses demonstrated how this mental fixation can profoundly impact the athlete's efforts. By excessively dwelling on his mistakes, Ashton narrowed his focus on rectifying errors, overlooking the broader part of his game that required attention. This fixation not only affected his practice routine but also led to increased pressure and stress, staying with him for future games.

Picture the last time you made a mistake in sport—a missed shot, a fumble, or a critical error. Did that moment replay in your mind, almost like an endless loop, long after it was over? Our thoughts and feelings glue themselves to us, making us believe we are what we think. In sports, this can be both a friend and a foe. Sometimes, we get so entangled in our thoughts and emotions that they control us, affecting our game and confidence. For example, a missed penalty in soccer might become, "I can't believe I missed that penalty kick. That was such a rookie error. Everyone will think I'm hopeless." Can you see that the athlete has generalized one error to being "hopeless" and assumed they know what everyone (whoever they are) will think! It seems an obvious faulty thought when laid out, but how easy is it to fall into the same trap?

In competitive sports, being "fused" with our thoughts means getting stuck in a loop of replaying mistakes or dwelling excessively on losses. Despite numerous victories, Ashton gets absorbed in thoughts of his losses, dwelling on specific errors. His inner coach repeatedly reminds him of those mistakes, leading to feelings of embarrassment and regret, affecting his confidence and training.

That's where the idea of "defusion" is useful. It's a technique backed by solid science that helps us separate from these sticky thoughts and emotions, giving us space to see them for what they are —stories we tell ourselves, not always facts. Defusion is a crucial technique in sports psychology to change our relationship with thoughts and emotions. Think of it as loosening thoughts and feelings' grip on our actions and emotions. For athletes like Ashton, who tend to fixate on past losses and mistakes, defusion is about breaking free from being fused or stuck with those negative thoughts and feelings that hinder achievements.

Defusion introduces a technique to create mental distance from these thoughts and feelings. It's about gaining psychological space, allowing athletes like Ashton to observe their thoughts and emotions without being consumed by them. It's like stepping back and acknowledging these thoughts as passing ideas in the mind rather than absolute truths. By practicing defusion, athletes can learn to recognize these thoughts and emotions without letting them dictate their actions, feelings, or practice routines.

Ashton can practice defusion by recognizing that thoughts about specific mistakes in a race, don't define his overall ability as a cross-country runner. His inner coach can help him observe these thoughts without letting them affect his practice or confidence. The inner coach might say, "Ashton, those thoughts about the errors are just thoughts. They're not the whole story, and they don't determine your ability. Let's acknowledge them and then refocus on the next race." This approach allows Ashton to separate himself from the specific negative thoughts and focus on improvement without dwelling on past setbacks. By practicing defusion, your thinking becomes clearer and more realistic and forgiving.

So, what can you do to give yourself more "space" from your thoughts and feelings?

Labeling thoughts: Labeling thoughts involves mentally categorizing them without judgment. For instance, during a tennis match, if a player notices critical thoughts like "I'm going to miss this serve," they can acknowledge it as an "unhelpful thought" without getting caught up in its content.

Takeaway action: Practice labeling thoughts regularly during training sessions. When thoughts arise, categorize them as "helpful" or "unhelpful" to create distance from their impact on your performance.

Focused action: Focused action directs attention to specific, actionable cues. For example, a sprinter may focus on arm swing and foot placement during a race, redirecting attention from nervousness about the competition's outcome to executing fundamental techniques.

Takeaway action: Prioritize a singular, performance-related action during crucial moments in practice or competition. This approach can reduce anxiety and improve execution by anchoring focus on controllable elements.

Acceptance strategies: Acceptance involves acknowledging and allowing thoughts and emotions without attempting to control them. Prior to a soccer match, an athlete might acknowledge feelings of pressure or stress as natural reactions without trying to change them, "I notice I have butterflies in my stomach." The concept of acceptance is simply to observe the feeling without attempting to alter it; noticing it is enough.

Takeaway action: Practice mindfulness techniques regularly to cultivate acceptance. Engage in activities like deep breathing or body scans to accept emotions and thoughts.

Grounding techniques: Grounding techniques utilize the senses (sight, sound, touch, smell, or taste) to anchor in the present moment. For instance, a basketball player might focus on the sensation of the ball in their hands, or a swimmer might listen to the sound of their breathing to stay present behind the blocks.

Takeaway action: Develop a pre-game routine incorporating grounding techniques. Use sensory cues like touch or breath awareness to anchor focus and reduce distractions during critical moments. Your senses will bring you back to the present and help you to do the required actions of the moment.

Engage with your inner coach: Have you ever noticed that it's often easier to give advice to others, rather than yourself?! During training, imagine your inner coach providing supportive advice or encouragement, fostering a positive mindset. By having a conversation with your inner coach, you will view your situation with more clarity, ultimately leading to better decision-making. Here's an example of what your inner coach might say, "I'm noticing nervousness before this big game, but I know I've prepared well. Think of all the hard work I've put in and the progress I've made. I've faced tough situations before, and I've come out stronger. I can do this. I just need to focus on my game plan and trust in my abilities. Let's do this!"

Takeaway action: Regularly talk with your inner coach in moments of doubt or stress. Create a mental conversation that offers constructive feedback or reassurance during challenging situations.

Practice regularly: Consistent practice of mental strategies helps integrate them into routines. Allocate specific training sessions to mindfulness, visualization, or mental rehearsal, gradually increasing frequency and duration.

Takeaway action: Incorporate mental skill sessions into your training schedule consistently. Make mental practice a priority to strengthen these techniques and improve their effectiveness over time. Consider keeping a record of your mental training and progress as part of your journaling.

The story of Ashton underscores the fine balance between acknowledging areas for improvement and becoming overwhelmed by the negativity bias. His experience highlights the importance of striking that balance—using setbacks as learning opportunities without allowing them to overshadow achievements. It serves as a reminder that dwelling excessively on mistakes can impede progress and cloud judgment, preventing you from moving forward with clarity and confidence.

It's important to understand that building your mental toughness involves taking a balanced perspective to overcome negativity bias. Recognizing the impact of this bias and applying strategies discussed in this chapter—such as mindfulness, mental reframing, and constructive feedback—is crucial. By doing so, you can learn from setbacks without becoming overwhelmed, fostering a mindset that propels you forward in your journey. Ashton's story underscores the importance of finding balance between learning from the past and moving forward with a helpful mindset, both in sports and in life. Integrating these practices into your routines will not only improve your performance but also your state of mind, setting you apart from others.

Journal prompt

Review the strategies provided for managing intrusive thoughts and choose one. Consider how you could implement this technique for your own benefit. Utilize your journal to outline your upcoming actions and evaluate their effectiveness. You can revisit alternative strategies later if you wish.

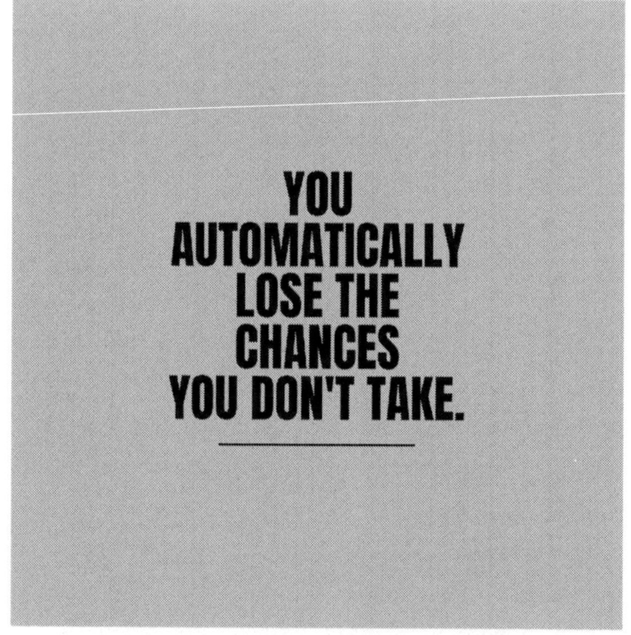

YOU
AUTOMATICALLY
LOSE THE
CHANCES
YOU DON'T TAKE.

CHAPTER EIGHT
TRIUMPH OVER TRIALS

"Optimism is the faith that leads to achievement. Nothing can be done without hope and confidence."
Helen Keller

HOPE IGNITES: THE FOUNDATION OF OPTIMISM

"Hope is NOT a strategy." I vividly remember the first time I heard those words, particularly because they were directed straight at me! Words spoken from the back of a room in a loud and forceful voice with over 150 people in attendance. I was delivering a workshop, and the topic was the relationship between optimism and high performance. Spoiler alert—optimism is a game-changer. Optimism is the tendency to view every cloud with a silver lining. It is the ability to take adversity and find a helpful way to consider the situation moving forward. I am a fan of analogies; they make sense to me. So, in explaining optimism and pessimism (think: every silver lining has a cloud!) I often use a sunglasses analogy. Imagine you have two pairs of sunglasses, one pair of dark shades, and one pair of bright pink. When you put on dark sunglasses, it clouds your vision and may make it difficult to see; the pink, in contrast, offers you a brighter picture, literally rose-colored glasses. We can put either of these glasses on, but for most of us we get used to the one pair of glasses, and tend to wear them most of the time.

We were in the workshop, and the audience was a large group of educators. I enjoy speaking with groups of professionals, an audience that is open to sharing their views and having robust conversations. I had spoken about viewing the world along the continuum of "Eeyore" through to "Tigger" (for those familiar with the 100-Acre Wood). For the Eeyores of the world life is a struggle, if something hasn't gone wrong, it will—soon. In contrast for the world's Tiggers, there are future possibilities, something to look forward to, a reason to smile, and a general expectation that things will go well.

I summarised key findings from hundreds of studies showing how a person might explain the world matters greatly. I had just explained that optimism and pessimism could be one of the most significant factors for people regarding career success, health outcomes, sporting performance, healthy relationships, and educational achievements. Optimism is an absolute winner in the competitive world. As a habitual thinking style, we can do many important things to push ourselves up and down the continuum, depending on our thoughts.

As I shared with the audience, optimism is generally considered to have four key elements. It starts with personalization. When you experience success or disappointment, how likely are you to attribute it to yourself? Confidence is built when we understand success comes from within. When we create great outcomes, we can (and should) acknowledge some of that credit, the "Yay-me" moments. Enjoy them when they come.

In contrast, disappointment looks realistically across all factors influencing the outcome. Your performance in the game will be affected by the actions of your teammates, weather conditions, ability of the opposition, etc. Optimistic personalization recognizes individual responsibility for success and understands that disappointments arise from many influences, not all of them due to the individual.

The second is pervasiveness. How far does your success "spill" into other areas? Consider the difference between asserting, "I am good at a right-handed layup," vs. "I do well in my offensive plays." Similarly, when a disappointment arises, "I need to improve my free throws" vs. "I am a terrible shooter." Optimistic pervasiveness looks broadly when you've done well, specifically when interpreting disappointment. Pessimistic pervasiveness does that in reverse—disappointment reflects your bigger picture, and success is simply due to a specific reason that may not permeate other skill areas.

The third important element of optimism (and if you guessed it is another "p" word, you would be right) is permanence. How long is the cause of this result likely to last? Our ability to refine a skill is usually long-lasting, so to be poor with the long pass means it's expected to be inadequate for some time. In contrast, poor effort may reflect a day, an hour, or even a passage of play. One sticks around, while the other can change rapidly.

Until now, the audience was nodding, and the combination of personalization, pervasiveness, and permanence was making sense. The final part of the puzzle for me to introduce was what lies at the foundation of the three "P's" . . . hope. The research of Martin Seligman (and many of his colleagues) strongly argues that hope is the cornerstone of optimism. It fosters helpful expectations and possibilities, shaping your perspective and making tough moments easier to handle. This understanding allows you to endure hardships, knowing that brighter days lie ahead.

At that moment, the hand was raised from the back of the room. "Hope is not a strategy. It doesn't do us any good to tell us to be hopeful because that won't change what's happening. I tell my students all the time, hope is not a strategy." The heads in the room quickly spun around to look at me and see how I would respond to such a statement. I like being challenged in a presentation. It tells me that the topic is important, and I have participants sufficiently engaged to offer an alternative point of view. In this instance, our views weren't oppositional, as I agreed with her statement. I would say that many people use hope as part of their thinking; people hope for things all the time: "I hope I pass my driving test," "I hope I get picked for the team," "I hope we win." Where hope becomes a challenge is when you use it as your sole strategy. "I am going to hope I get picked for the team and not do anything extra," "I am going to hope the exam questions are easy and not do much study." I don't recommend being hopeful as your *only* path forward. Still, I argue it is a useful approach to a situation when you've done all you can. For example, you have completed all your driving lessons, driven the course with the instructor and you can also hope you don't get the "mean" examiner everyone warned you about—but trust you will be okay if you do! It's also okay to do all the set training, review video footage on how to improve your tactical knowledge, ask questions of coaches, and then also hope that when the team sheet comes out that your name is on it.

Hope is a mental approach (or framework) that can help you through the time when you are awaiting an outcome (sitting in the test car just before the instructor tells you if you've passed or waiting for 2 pm when the team list will be shared). So, while hope is a strategy, it works more effectively when it's an approach to thinking, and you have other plans to back you up.

THE INESCAPABLE TRUTH ABOUT IGNORING THOUGHTS: WHY YOU CAN'T JUST "BLOCK IT OUT"

Jackie was a 27-year-old powerlifter who had been training for months to compete in the upcoming regional powerlifting competition. She had a rigorous training schedule and was determined to win. However, in the days leading up to the event, Jackie thought about a twinge in her lower back. She didn't actually feel anything she just thought about it in a way of wondering about the possibility of an injury.

Despite her efforts to ignore the thoughts and "block it out," Jackie found that her concerns about a possible injury were starting to affect her training. She couldn't focus on her lifts, and her normally precise technique started slipping.

Jackie asked for my advice on how to deal with her anxiety. During our conversation, she said she had been trying to block out her worries, but that wasn't working. I then explained to Jackie that trying to ignore her fears wasn't the solution; in fact, it would most likely make it worse.

Trying to block out negative thoughts can be counterproductive, making them even more persistent and difficult to ignore. When we try to suppress thoughts, we actually pay more attention to them, and they can become more intrusive and bothersome. Blocking out a thought is akin to trying to hold a buoy underwater: initially manageable, but as pressure builds, it becomes increasingly challenging to contain. Just like the buoy's force pushing against our hands, the more one tries to suppress a thought, the more it demands our attention, and the stronger it may resurface, popping up high above the water.

In contrast, acknowledging and accepting negative thoughts is a more effective strategy. This means acknowledging the thought without trying to fight it or push it away. Instead, it involves observing the thought without judgment and allowing it to pass without getting attached.

Research has shown that this approach, known as mindful attention, can help reduce the impact of negative thoughts on our emotions and behavior. Acknowledging and accepting negative thoughts can reduce their power over us and help us to develop greater resilience and emotional regulation. Owning thoughts is akin to shining a light on shadows in a dark room. When you acknowledge a thought, it's like illuminating it; suddenly, it becomes clearer and less intimidating. Much like how shadows dissipate when exposed to light, acknowledging thoughts diminishes their power, making them more manageable and less overwhelming.

Instead of blocking out negative thoughts, practicing accepting them and letting them go without getting caught up is better. The earlier described strategy of delusion is a helpful way to do this. This can become a natural habit with practice, and we can learn to manage our negative thoughts more effectively, leading to improved mental health and well-being.

One strategy that may be helpful for you is to practice accepting and visualizing your negative thoughts. Instead of trying to block them out or push them away, try acknowledging their presence and allowing them to exist without judgment. Visualize your negative thoughts as something you can control with an imaginary dial. You can turn down the volume or change the color to black and white, for example, to reduce the intensity of the thought. This can help you manage the anxiety you're feeling and make it easier to focus on your training and preparation for the competition. I have had athletes visualize the words written down on paper, seeing the letters. Another athlete I worked with used to see the words formed as letters in the sky, like the ones you might see a plane carve into the sky.

Then, imagine dissolving the thought so it disappears, freeing yourself from its grip. Doing this can reduce the power of negative thoughts on your emotions and behavior and increase your resilience and emotional regulation. The letters could disappear from the paper; the sky could turn blue as the letters dissolve.

In our subsequent sessions, Jackie began implementing the technique of acknowledging and accepting her unhelpful self-talk. When the worry about her lower back crept in during training, she consciously recognized the thought without judgment. Instead of attempting to push it away, she acknowledged the concern, saying, "Okay, I notice this worry about my lower back right now, and that's okay. It's a thought, not something that really exists. I'll tell the trainer —it's their worry, not mine."

Over time, Jackie started noticing a shift in her mindset. She gradually reduced their influence over her by acknowledging her worries without resisting or magnifying them. This newfound approach allowed her to train with greater focus and confidence. As she continued to apply the technique consistently, Jackie found that the power of her anxieties diminished. By accepting her thoughts as passing events rather than absolute truths, she regained control over her mental state. Eventually, when the competition day arrived, Jackie could step onto the platform with a clearer mind, demonstrating her skill and technique with confidence, unencumbered by the fear of an impending injury. Her progress highlighted the transformative effect of acknowledging and accepting unhelpful thoughts, empowering her to perform at her best.

This strategy may take some practice, but it can become a natural and effective habit for managing negative thoughts with time and repetition. Let your inner coach help you to find the strategy that will make the most sense to you. Don't think of imaginary letters in the sky if that feels silly; find something that works. It may be the self-talk appearing on your phone to which you then hit the delete button to make it disappear! Try incorporating it into your daily routine in the weeks leading up to the competition and see how it works. Remember, it's important to be patient and give yourself time to master this technique.

MATCH POINT EMOTIONS: DECODING THE THIN LINE BETWEEN TENNIS NERVES AND EXCITEMENT

Dakota, a rising tennis star, had been preparing vigorously for the upcoming championship match. This event was crucial in defining her next opportunity on the circuit. As the match day approached, Dakota experienced a roller-coaster of emotions that left her unsettled. She noticed that her physical symptoms seemed to fluctuate, swinging between excitement and worry, akin to the rhythm of a tennis ball being volleyed across the court.

In the days leading up to the match, Dakota noticed a flurry of physical sensations. Her heart raced, her palms became sweaty, and she felt a knot in her stomach—typical indicators of anxiety and worry. However, intertwined with these sensations was an undeniable surge of excitement. Dakota's mind flipped backwards and forwards between anxious apprehension and exhilarating anticipation.

The morning of the match arrived and as Dakota woke up, her heart was pounding, her breaths were shallow, and her mind was filled with thoughts of success and failure. She was very aware that her physiology was activated but was torn between wanting to leap out of bed to start the day or pull the covers over her head!

Dakota's inner coach took a moment to reflect on the similarity of her physical symptoms between worry and excitement. She realized her body's anxious or thrilled reactions were the same. Her racing heart and adrenaline rush felt the same as times when she had been really anxious and really excited. Drawing from this realization, Dakota began to rethink her situation. She recognized that her body's response was not only an indicator of fear but also a sign of heightened arousal and readiness. In that moment she realised that the boundary between worry and excitement was thin, and often, worry could be a disguised form of excitement.

With this revelation, Dakota reframed her pre-match nerves. Instead of viewing her symptoms solely as anxiety, she began to perceive them as signs of excitement and readiness to perform at her best. She adopted positive self-talk and reminded herself that her energy, blended with nerves and enthusiasm, was essential for her peak performance. Dakota's realization that worries and excitement share similar physical sensations was critical in her high-achievement journey. Understanding how emotions and physiology interact together is the first step in taking control of feelings to impact your performance.

I realized this distinction once when standing in line with my then 8-year-old for a ride on a roller coaster! Two people, standing together about to go on the same exciting/terrifying adventure. And right there is the distinction: is it exciting or scary? Whatever the interpretation, the reality is the same—two people getting on a roller coaster and having the same *physical* experience. It's the *psychological* interpretation that dramatically differentiates the experience.

When I am about to do something well out of my comfort zone, one of my go-to strategies is to remind myself that sometimes the worry I notice may be *excitement in disguise*. That helps. It stops me from getting on the worry train and getting stuck on it. The possibility that something is exciting about this situation can be enough to help me exhale, relax, and calm my thinking to be more helpful. I also think about the problem and make myself finish the sentence that starts with, "How good! I am about to . . ."

"How good! I am about to get more experience performing in front of a big crowd."
"How good! I am about to practice my media skills by doing this interview."
"How good! I am about to test my ability against a great opposition."
"How good! I will try out that new play/skill/technique."
"How good! I get to race in a final."

The sentence frames the experience through the emotion of energy and excitement rather than worry and apprehension. Let's see how this played out for Dakota.

As Dakota stepped onto the court, she felt emotions wash over her. Her heart raced, and her palms were sweaty, but she welcomed these sensations this time. "How good! It's time to shine in the championship game." She played with a newfound sense of freedom, channeling the combination of worry and excitement into her game. The match unfolded, and Dakota performed remarkably well, securing victory in a closely contested battle.

Post-match, Dakota reflected on her journey and the lesson she had learned. She understood that the interpretation of her emotions played a pivotal role. By acknowledging that worry and excitement shared similar physical signs, she changed her perception of nerves into a tool for a powerful performance.

Dakota's experience in understanding the influence of emotions adjusted her approach to important matches and became a valuable lesson in embracing nervousness as a source of positive energy. Her story underscores the importance of managing emotions and harnessing their potential for optimal performance.

The next time you are in an anxiety-provoking situation, consider if excitement and opportunity might also be underlying the scenario. Is this physical activation you are experiencing simply excitement in disguise?

BELIEF IN ACTION: HOW CUE WORDS CAN SET YOU UP FOR SUCCESS

Cooper was an elite basketball player who was quickly moving up through the ranks within his team. From bench player to occasional starting five, he got opportunities faster than expected during the season. His coach had given him some feedback on areas for improvement, including taking more time when he comes off a screen. He was moving too quickly, and being rushed, which meant he was making errors and forcing teammates to be out of position for the play.

When we talked about his positioning, he said he was aware after the fact but found it difficult to remember to slow down in the heat of play. We used the when/then habit formation strategy to automate coming off the screen slower and more in control. In a nutshell, the when/then strategy requires you to identify a trigger action (already in place) that you pair with the new behavior you wish to include. In this instance, the "when" is the trigger of going into a screen. After a discussion with Cooper, I recommended he create a "cue" word that represented moving slower and with purpose (the "then"). The word he chose was "smooth." The strategy now becomes:

When . . . I go into the screen . . . then . . . I think "smooth."

It took a game and a couple of practice sessions, with Cooper setting the phrase as a goal before training sessions and reviewing it after practice. Soon, the word became automated and the actions he wanted followed.

The importance of habits is a key message in *The Elite: Think like an athlete, succeed like a champion.* Within Chapter 3 of that book, I outline why habits are critical to success and the when/then strategy to create new habits (and break old ones). If you'd like to understand habit formation in more detail, I recommend you re-read that chapter from *The Elite* (available through my website or online if you don't have a copy).

Cue words can be powerful tools within elite performance. Your words are closely linked to defining how you feel, so the right word can elevate or calm you in a way that sets you up for performance. Finding the right cue word as a trigger is a personal preference, and I encourage you to experiment with how words lead you to feel at any given moment. Below are examples of cue words and suggestions for how they can make you think. Don't worry if you experience them differently—your interpretation is the only one that matters!

If you want to feel . . .
Calmer . . . *try this cue word* . . . Smooth
Higher arousal . . . *try this cue word* . . . Flow
Excited . . . *try this cue word* . . . Snap
In control . . . *try this cue word* . . . Precision
Momentum . . . *try this cue word* . . . Energy
Clarity . . . *try this cue word* . . . Focus

Some words you will be drawn to, others won't work for you. I encourage you to find a couple of phrases that work for you, practice them, try them in competition, and use them as tools to shift your feelings when necessary.

THE RAPID DISPOSAL METHOD: ELIMINATING UNHELPFUL THOUGHTS

The next strategy might only resonate with some, but it's worth sharing because of its effectiveness. Picture this: you're in a washroom, tissue in hand. You drop it into the bowl, press a button, and whoosh! It vanishes. Now, switch that scenario to your field of play—the court, the track, the stadium, or wherever your sport takes you. A negative, unhelpful thought barges in just as you're about to perform. It's intrusive, like a spark in dry tinder. Giving it attention only fuels its flame. So, the best move? You need to move on swiftly. Imagine that negative thought as words on a tissue dropped into a bowl—now hit that flush button! Zoom, it's gone.

The athletes I work with affectionately know this as the "flush it" strategy. Yes, the washroom imagery might not suit everyone's taste, but it's undeniably effective. Athletes have discussed and successfully applied this technique within a single session. It's a vivid and impactful image; flushing something away signifies swift, powerful movement. This strategy particularly shines in moments requiring immediate action.

The rapid disposal method is a mental exercise that with practice can assist you to master the art of instant thought dismissal. When confronted with negativity, visualize the unwanted thought as a piece of paper with words inscribed. Mentally drop this "paper" into the "bowl" of your mind and swiftly press the "flush button." The key lies in associating this visual imagery with the prompt action of the flush to discard the thought.

To implement this technique effectively:

Visualization practice: Before competitions or training, practice mental rehearsals where you visualize this flushing action vividly. Connect by pressing the flush button to remove the negative thought swiftly.

Immediate action: As soon as an unhelpful thought arises, don't dwell on it. Immediately execute the mental action of dropping it into the "bowl" and hitting the "flush button."

Repetition and consistency: Like any skill, repetition is vital. Regularly practice this mental flush exercise in various scenarios to reinforce its effectiveness and make it a habit.

Post-flush focus: After "flushing" the thought, redirect your attention to the present moment or an affirmative mental cue, such as a phrase or an image representing positivity or focus in your sport.

Reflection and adjustment: Reflect on instances where this technique worked and where it might need refinement. Adjust the mental imagery or the execution method to suit your mental landscape better.

Mastering the rapid disposal method involves swiftly training your mind to recognize and dispose of unproductive thoughts. Consistent practice and intentional application during crucial moments in your sporting endeavors will gradually solidify this mental skill, empowering you to maintain focus, resilience, and peak performance.

Let's focus on a crucial aspect of your athletic journey: this is a pivotal moment where your choices carry significant weight. You're in control here—will you unwittingly become your own toughest opponent or consciously stand as your greatest supporter? Amidst the critics and doubters, there's a powerful yet often overlooked voice within: your inner coach. This internal critic can flood you with negative, self-limiting thoughts, like unwanted guests overstaying their welcome in your mental space.

Imagine your mind as a prized arena, limited but precious. Every thought, whether empowering or self-defeating, competes for a spot in this valuable space. Negative thoughts, like unwelcome intruders, disrupt this mental turf, impeding your progress and stifling your potential. It's time to take back control—to evict these destructive tenants and upgrade your inner coach to champion your aspirations.

Journal prompt

Browse through this chapter and pick out a single idea that captures your attention the most. How can you connect this idea to your athletic endeavors? What specific action will you take to incorporate this idea into your sport experience?

Becoming your most steadfast advocate is a game-changer. If you can't wholeheartedly support your skills and resilience, how can you expect the world to rally behind you? External validation and support stem from your unwavering belief in and endorsement of your abilities. Sometimes, the path to victory requires stepping back and allowing your most empowering self to take the lead—guiding you toward your athletic peak.

You create a mental fortress primed for success, perseverance, and unshakeable confidence by freeing your mind from unhelpful self-talk. Embrace the idea of championing yourself, cultivating a mindset deeply rooted in clear and helpful thinking. Witness it become the foundation of your rise in championship thinking within your sport and in life's broader arena.

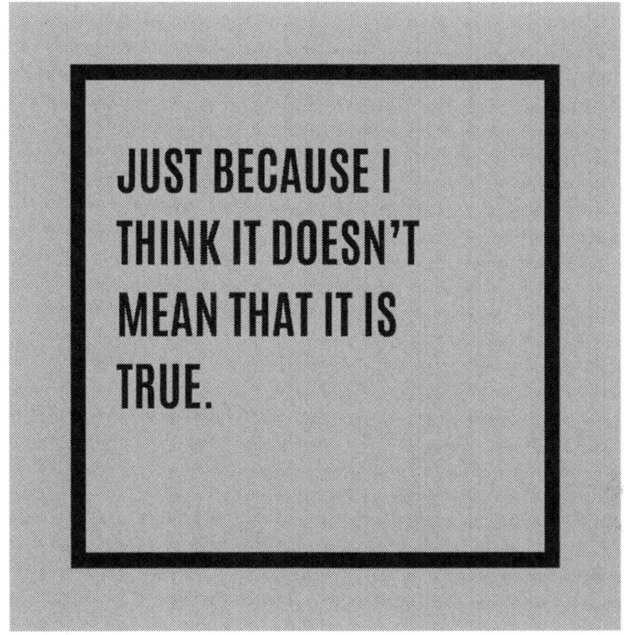
JUST BECAUSE I
THINK IT DOESN'T
MEAN THAT IT IS
TRUE.

CHAPTER NINE
EMOTIONAL RESILIENCE FOR PEAK PERFORMANCE

"Strength and growth come only through continuous effort and struggle."
Napoleon Hill

HAVE you ever watched the movie "Inside-Out"? It's a fun animated film that peeks into the life of a young tween, Riley, and her family, but more than pure entertainment, it delves deep into the emotions that govern their experiences. Imagine, these emotions—Fear, Joy, Disgust, Sadness, and Anger—are like a tight-knit team stationed at a control panel within the minds.

As athletes, emotions are our companions throughout our sporting journey. That jittery flutter of Fear before a crucial match, the exhilarating rush of Joy that follows a hard-earned victory, the pang of Disgust when things don't quite go as planned, or the subtle hint of Sadness after a tough loss—these emotions are part and parcel of the experience.

This chapter looks at these emotions, diving into practical insights on how to navigate and leverage them to your advantage in your athletic endeavors.

EMBRACING SORROW: THE UNEXPECTED POWER OF SADNESS

Austin, a skilled baseball player, experienced a difficult season marked by ongoing sporting and personal challenges. The recent loss of a loved one and a painful breakup weighed heavily upon him. He found it difficult to sleep, and harder to get out of bed. Not normally one to cry, he would suddenly find himself getting teary at moments that wouldn't normally affect him. His playing suffered and his coaches and teammates started to notice his change in demeanor and drop in performances. With each error and defeat on the diamond, frustration mounted, and Austin felt as though everything was going wrong, unable to catch a break.

In the realm of athletic endeavor, emotions play a pivotal role. Among this, sadness stands as a formidable yet often misunderstood emotion. Delving into the nature and impact of sorrow is important as life is full of sad instances, and knowing how to manage yourself during those times is important.

Sadness is a fundamental human emotion that can stem from personal experiences, adversity, and the feeling when we have experienced loss. It presents not only as a response to immediate setbacks, but also as a reaction to emotionally charged situations such as injury, facing the disappointment of missing out on crucial team selections, or unmet personal achievement. When confronted with these instances of grief, sadness can become a substantial obstacle, likely to impede an athlete's progress.

Research highlights that sadness, unlike many other emotions, can slow an athlete's momentum. It acts like an anchor, reducing motivation, stifling enthusiasm, and clouding the mental clarity necessary to train and compete. In times of difficulty, this emotion can become a formidable adversary, hindering an athlete's ability to rebound swiftly and re-engage with their athletic pursuits.

However, within the realm of sporting challenges and personal setbacks lies a reality that initially may feel difficult to comprehend—the beneficial potential of sadness. Despite its propensity to slow us down, sadness, when understood and channeled well, can prompt change, learning, and improvement.

Determined to turn things around, Austin was desperate to find a way to get back on top of his sport and his life. Austin spoke to the team psychologist about his personal circumstances and sporting frustrations. This change in approach prompted Austin to understand sadness better and what to do when it is strong in your life. He recognized that sadness is your mind's way of telling you that something was important to you, and that the feeling is not only normal but part of being human. Being sad gave him time to talk and think about what was important in his life and how he wanted things to be moving forward.

Our inner coach can help us to understand our underlying reasons for the emotions we are experiencing. Embracing sadness as a guidepost rather than a stop sign opens avenues for self-discovery, resilience-building, and adaptive coping mechanisms.

Further, whilst we'd all rather avoid sad times, sadness can spark positive change. This emotion can push athletes to take significant steps forward when handled well. It ignites a stronger drive and motivates them to strive for excellence. Sadness becomes a powerful tool for self-motivation, encouraging athletes to find new ways of doing things, improve their game plans, and build mental strength in their sports pursuits.

In essence, while sadness may slow us down in moments of grief or disappointment, with the help of the inner coach, we can learn to understand ourselves better and make decisions for our future. Embracing this emotion as an opportunity for growth ultimately builds resilience and adaptive skills necessary to thrive amidst the challenges inherent in pursuing sporting excellence.

FROM DISGUST TO DISCOVERY

Disgust, in its various forms, can permeate both our physical and mental realms, often arriving uninvited and leaving an unmissable impression. Allow me to take you back to a vivid cycling escapade with friends that brought this emotion to the forefront. Picture us pedaling along an early morning route, the road dimly lit and our spirits high. Suddenly, the lead rider's sharp intake of breath signaled something amiss. Within moments, a palpable wave of disgust swept through the group. It was that primal instinct—a heightened awareness that something foul lurked nearby. Instinctively, the lead rider veered, deftly maneuvering to avoid a collision with a decaying Australian kangaroo sprawled on the road. Alas, not everyone in our group had the same forewarning. One rider, caught off guard, collided with the unfortunate creature. In the relentless heat of the Australian sun, the decomposing kangaroo had swollen with internal gases, morphing into an unsettling semblance of a grotesque balloon. Upon impact, it ruptured, drenching three riders in a putrid, stomach-churning sludge. Trust me, mere words can hardly encapsulate the full force of that repugnant odor! As I write these words, I can still smell it! If you found yourself involuntarily crinkling your nose while reading this, you've shared in the absolute disgust we all encountered that memorable day (apologies for the vivid recollection!).

The role of disgust as a protective mechanism against physical dangers is quite evident: avoiding road hazards or refraining from consuming spoiled food or drink. However, the intriguing facet of disgust extends into our psychological and interpersonal realms. Have you ever encountered behavior that makes your skin crawl? Witnessing someone casually discard chewing gum or spit it out in front of you might evoke an instinctual, visceral aversion. Amidst the revulsion, there's a valuable lesson if you take a moment to reflect. Disgust often illuminates our values, shining a light on what truly matters to us—typically the antithesis of what repulses us.

Let's delve into specific scenarios that often provoke feelings of disgust: witnessing someone carelessly littering, observing a player taking shortcuts, seeing a coach harshly berating a player for an error, or a teammate shirking drills and offering flimsy excuses. A common thread weaves through these instances—respect. Conflict often arises from perceived disrespect, and witnessing such behavior can provoke a strong sense of disgust. I view disgust as a psychological "call to action." Just as I would dispose of spoiled milk, if a teammate flouts training rules, I'd address the need to discuss it with them. Otherwise, it would further add to my discomfort. Reflecting on how disgust can fuel personal and collective growth is a powerful way to harness this emotion for improvement and progress.

Allow me to share an anecdote that captures this point: I once entered a sports complex alongside the team captain. As we walked he noticed some litter that had blown onto the field. Excusing himself momentarily, he scaled the fence and retrieved the rubbish, disposing of it in a nearby bin. Interested in his action, I asked him about it. His response was enlightening: "Jo, the grounds staff work tirelessly to maintain these field's. It's only fair that we show our gratitude and assist them in keeping it tidy." For him, to walk past rubbish was inconceivable. It's no surprise he was an exemplary captain, both on and off the field, embodying the essence of respect in every action.

FEARLESS LEAPS: MASTERING ANXIETY IN ATHLETICS

Jack, a talented high jump athlete, hails from a family with a history of worriers, an inheritance that influences his mental view. He candidly describes himself as constantly accompanied by an inexplicable sense of worry, an underlying feeling of unease that shadows his daily life. Jack finds it challenging to pinpoint the exact origins of this thinking despite his efforts.

Alongside this lingering unease, Jack experiences triggers that often manifest into episodes resembling panic attacks. Contemplating the prospect of failure triggers an overwhelming cascade of emotions within him. Waves of intensity surge through his body—his heart races, adrenaline courses through his veins, his palms grow damp with sweat, and taking deep breaths becomes arduous. These distressing physical sensations frequently prompt Jack to wonder if his experiences align with the symptoms he's encountered in descriptions by his peers and on social media platforms.

Jack's narrative portrays an athlete grappling with persistent emotional turmoil, a perpetual sense of apprehension, and confronting moments of heightened distress. As a high jump athlete aiming for excellence, understanding, and addressing Jack's particular experience of anxiety is crucial in providing him with the support and strategies necessary to navigate and manage these overwhelming emotions effectively.

Anxiety exists. Recognized as a treatable condition, anxiety is a psychological experience that a qualified medical and health professional best diagnoses. Importantly, anxiety is a treatable condition. In addition to the *psychological condition* of anxiety is the *feeling* of anxiety. Notice the difference highlighted in the previous sentence. Anxiety is the condition versus the feeling of anxiety. Feelings are transient. They come and go, like clouds across the sky or buses in a busy city. No sooner is one bus in front of you than another is passing by. Why the bus and cloud analogies? Well, because emotions and feelings can act the same way. Sitting strongly with us for a moment, then suddenly moving on. Importantly, while feeling anxious is normal, athletes have told me that feeling anxious makes them feel unprepared or weak. The good news is there are ways to manage the feelings of anxiety, and like other emotions, it can be changed quickly when you know how. I want to challenge your thinking that instead of avoiding or stepping away from anxiety, we may benefit from getting closer to it.

We're equipped with effective methods for handling these waves of anxiety. As you adjust your approach during a game, you can adapt your emotional response. Surprisingly, rather than evading anxiety like an opponent, there's merit in confronting it directly. I know it might sound unconventional but consider this: when you face your anxiety head-on, you can reduce its intensity and discover your own reserves of strength.

Remember, excelling as an athlete often involves overcoming

challenges. Fear, in a way, resembles a training partner that pushes you to exceed your limits. In the upcoming chapters, we'll explore effective strategies for managing fear and channeling its energy to enhance your performance. Think of it as refining your mental resilience, and using fear as part of your mental arsenal, rather than your opposition.

Prepare to transform nervous energy into a secret weapon that propels you forward. So how, then, do we manage anxiety or the feeling of anxiety? Understanding that fear is a normal human emotion is part of learning how to manage it. Being fearful can be a sign of the importance of an experience.

RAGING STORMS AND CALM SEAS: THE HIGHS AND LOWS OF ANGER

Adam is an accomplished golf player known for his precision and skill on the course. Adam's game is often a stark contrast between his strong performances and the psychological toll of overreactions to mistakes.

When Adam doesn't meet his high expectations, it sparks a wave of internal angst. Despite his mastery of the game, a missed putt or a seemingly poor club decision on the course deeply affects him. The frustration and disappointment from these instances often overtake his mental space, casting a shadow over subsequent shots and impacting his overall performance.

Adam's reactions become a struggle to regain focus and composure. His otherwise steady game can be significantly disrupted as he grapples with the mental challenge of overcoming even the smallest of setbacks. His friends refer to him as the 'Jeckyl and Hyde' of golf, smiling and laughing when things are going well; and moments later slamming his club in anger or becoming visibly tense and uptight after a poor shot. This mental barrier affects his current play and lingers, creeping into future matches and shaking his confidence and his scorecard on the greens.

As a golfer with great potential and skill, Adam's case highlights the vital connection between staying mentally sharp and delivering on sporting performance. Addressing these challenges is key to unlocking his full potential and ensuring that Adam's mental game aligns with his playing promise.

Anger, an intense and complex emotion, emerges from many triggers and experiences, particularly instances of lack of respect, disappointment, or embarrassment. When athletes face disrespectful behaviors from opponents, fail to meet personal or team performance goals, or commit errors detrimental to the team's success, anger can surface as a natural response. It can feel an instinctive reaction from perceived injustices or frustrations within the sporting context. Often misunderstood, anger can possess the potential to both propel and derail an athlete's journey toward success.

Yet, while anger can serve as a potent fuel, propelling athletes towards higher levels of performance when appropriately channeled, its uncontrolled expression risks sabotaging one's potential. When anger spirals out of control, athletes may be entangled in detrimental outcomes, hindering focus, impairing decision-making, and negatively affecting team dynamics.

Anger, often considered a primary emotion, can manifest as a secondary response triggered by underlying feelings such as fear, hurt, or vulnerability. In the high-stakes world of sports, athletes frequently encounter situations where the immediate display of fear may seem inconsistent with the expected demeanor or the desired image of strength and control. Consequently, this clash between the automatic response of anxiety and the personal expectations of composure in the face of adversity leads to the redirection of fear into anger.

Consider a basketball player in a high-pressure playoff game. In a critical moment, a series of missed shots and mounting pressure culminate in a turnover that costs the team a crucial possession. In the heat of the moment, the player feels a pang of fear and embarrassment for the error made in a game of such magnitude. However, adhering to the expectations of showcasing resilience and toughness, the immediate and visible emotion displayed is not fear or embarrassment but rather a burst of visible anger—pounding the ball in frustration or lashing out at teammates.

In this scenario, when expressed as anger, the fear of failure, embarrassment, or letting down teammates serves as a protective shield, concealing the underlying vulnerability and conveying strength or competitiveness in the heat of competition. The almost instantaneous switch from fear to anger exemplifies how athletes, constrained by expectations or personal pressure, bypass the primary emotion of fear, and instead exhibit anger.

Understanding the intricate relationship between fear and anger is an essential aspect of emotional management for athletes, and here, the role of the inner coach—our internal dialogue and self-evaluation—becomes pivotal. By training the inner coach to recognize fear as a potential precursor to anger, athletes can leverage this self-awareness to delve deeper into their emotional responses. Through reflection guided by the inner coach, athletes can unearth the root causes behind their emotions, facilitating a more authentic and constructive expression of their feelings within the competitive arena.

Comprehending anger's dynamics is a cornerstone for athletes seeking to harness its potential while avoiding its adverse effects. When the inner coach actively collaborates with you to understand and manage anger, it has the potential to result in positive change. It propels athletes to refocus their energies, intensify their determination, and rekindle their pursuit of excellence. Empowered by the inner coach, athletes can translate anger into a powerful force, encouraging them to initiate corrective actions, address performance setbacks, and cultivate resilience in adversity.

Effectively managing anger necessitates a multiple approach including self-awareness, emotional regulation, and strategic coping mechanisms—areas where the inner coach can play a pivotal role. By fostering a strong partnership between the inner coach and the athlete, tailored strategies can be developed to channel and redirect intense emotions constructively. Techniques like mindfulness, controlled breathing exercises, and cognitive reappraisal, through the guidance of the inner coach, serve as effective tools in diffusing anger, enhancing mental clarity, and empowering athletes to respond composedly in demanding situations.

In conclusion, while anger possesses the potential to both uplift and hinder an athlete's journey, understanding its origins, interplay with fear, and managing strategies hold the key to harnessing its benefits effectively. By developing a comprehensive approach towards anger , athletes can unlock their motivational potential while preserving their focus, resilience, and competitive edge in the dynamic realm of sports.

UNLOCKING MOMENTS: FINDING JOY IN EVERY CHALLENGE

Zach was a seasoned American football player known for his prowess on the field. Zach relied solely on grit and determination throughout his career, often pushing himself relentlessly to excel. However, an unexpected shift occurred when he learned to incorporate joy and gratitude into his performance.

Zach underwent a substantial change that altered his approach to the game. Initially, he considered football solely a battlefield where strength and strategy were paramount. The pressure to perform often consumed him, which sometimes led to unnecessary stress and decreased productivity. He was far from happy, and his performances felt like he was continually falling short, even when the team won.

Attending a mental conditioning session where he learned about the impact of joy and gratitude on performance turned his thinking around. He realized that finding happiness in every game and expressing appreciation for the opportunity to play the sport he loved could significantly enhance his performance.

By embracing joy, Zach tapped into a renewed enthusiasm on the field. He learned to savor the moments, enjoy the camaraderie of his teammates, the thrill of making a successful play, and even the lessons learned from mistakes. Additionally, Zach incorporated gratitude into his routine, expressing thankfulness for his team, coaches, and the chance to compete at such a high level.

This shift in mindset profoundly affected Zach's performance. He noticed increased mental clarity, enhanced focus, and an overall improvement in his gameplay. By including joy and gratitude into his approach, Zach discovered a newfound sense of satisfaction, leading to better performance and a more balanced and fulfilling athletic journey.

Joy is a dynamic emotion that can rejuvenate and inspire us. It often springs from personal victories or team achievements, providing confidence and motivation. However, when joy becomes all-encompassing—especially during a winning streak—it may divert our attention from the fundamental elements that initially led to success.

Joy evolves from triumph and competitive achievements, fostering fulfillment and camaraderie. Its positive aspects are a motivational booster, replenishing our mental reserves, and igniting our passion for sport.

Yet, an excess of joy during prolonged success can present challenges. Athletes might lose sight of the habits and focus that propelled them to victory. Amid celebration, there's a risk of becoming complacent and experiencing a decline in performance.

Effectively managing joy requires balance. While it's a remarkable source of motivation, it shouldn't overshadow the essential strategies that contributed to success. Athletes can maintain this equilibrium by staying connected with their inner coach—reflecting regularly on emotions, setting short-term goals, and cultivating a growth-oriented mindset. These practices act as guiding pillars amid the highs of joy, helping athletes remain focused on their long-term objectives.

Ultimately, joy in sports offers immense benefits alongside potential challenges. By embracing self-awareness, setting progressive goals, and engaging with the inner coach to navigate emotions, athletes can harness the positive aspects of joy while safeguarding against its potential distractions. This balanced approach ensures athletes stay focused, consistent, and successful in their sporting pursuits.

Emotions are akin to a team stationed at the control panel within our minds, guiding us through every athletic endeavor. Like Riley and her emotional team in "Inside-Out," you will navigate Fear, Joy, Disgust, Sadness, and Anger in your sporting experiences. Understanding the power of these emotions and harnessing their potential to drive your athletic performance is crucial. Too often I hear athletes speak of the controlling effects of their emotions. Your inner coach can assist you to be proactive in taking actions to adapt your emotions for success.

Embrace emotional agility: Remember, emotions aren't adversaries but valuable tools. Embrace the guidance of your inner coach. Utilize it to navigate and understand emotions like Sadness, Disgust, Anxiety, and Anger. Embrace Sadness as a catalyst for improvement, channel Disgust toward reflection, and manage Anxiety by confronting it. Anger can be an impetus for positive change when understood and channeled constructively.

Understanding dynamic emotions: Recognize the dynamics between emotions and performance. Emotional responses like Fear triggering Anger or Joy blurring focus during winning streaks can impact your sporting journey. Acknowledge the patterns, leverage the positives, and shield yourself from potential distractions.

Striking athletic balance: Achieving a balance between emotions and sporting success is key. Don't let one emotion overpower your focus. Use your inner coach to reflect, set achievable goals, and maintain a performance mindset. This balance ensures consistent performance and sustainable success.

Leveraging emotional awareness: Embrace your Emotional Intelligence (EQ) in sports. It's not about avoiding emotions but understanding and managing them effectively. Enhance self-awareness, regulate emotions, and employ coping mechanisms to navigate competitive pressure.

Gratitude and mindfulness in sport: Incorporate gratitude and mindfulness into your routine. When cultivating a grateful mindset, and practicing mindfulness you will increase your satisfaction, foster mental clarity, and enhance overall performance.

Self-reflection for athletic growth: Use setbacks as opportunities for self-reflection and improvement. Analyze what triggers your emotions. Develop strategies with your inner coach to address these triggers, enhancing resilience and adaptability in adversity.

Finding support in sports: Know when to seek support. If emotions become overwhelming or persistently impact your performance, seeking guidance from qualified professionals is beneficial. Embracing emotions doesn't mean dealing with them alone.

In essence, navigating emotions is an integral part of your athletic journey. Understanding emotions requires practice, patience, and dedication, like mastering any skill. Harnessing the power of emotions for sporting success involves understanding their complexity, leveraging their positives, and utilizing your inner coach as a guiding light in your pursuit of excellence on the field. You'll elevate your performance through self-awareness, balance, and effective management and discover a more fulfilling and rewarding athletic experience.

A WORD OF CAUTION

It's crucial to exercise caution when considering self-diagnosis in the pursuit of understanding your mental health. Recently, I encountered three athletes in a single week who believed they had experienced "panic attacks." Upon closer inquiry into their symptoms, it became evident that these episodes weren't panic attacks but rather moments of intense concern or worry. It's essential to recognize that worry is a natural and helpful emotion. It prompts us to exercise caution, heightens our awareness, and encourages us to proceed with greater care in various situations. When we interpret worry as valuable feedback, as data about our experiences, we harness its true benefits as part of our normal human experience.

It's important not to dismiss worry as an unproductive or negative emotion. Instead, when understood and managed effectively, worry becomes a helpful tool aiding our decision-making and responses. However, relying solely on social media platforms like TikTok for mental health advice might offer limited perspectives. It's advisable to seek a wider spectrum of information and guidance for a more comprehensive understanding.

Fortunately we now live in a time where the significance of mental health and the courage in speaking up are recognised. Strong emotions that raise concerns for you are worth discussing with a health professional. Your emotions drive your behaviours and are critical to your belief.

Journal prompt

Reflect on a recent challenging moment in your sport. How did you feel during that experience? What emotions arose, and how did you handle them? Consider what strategies helped you navigate those emotions effectively or what you could do differently next time to manage them better.

TOMORROW'S HAPPINESS WILL PAY FOR TODAY'S HARD WORK

CHAPTER TEN
MIND'S EYE MASTERY

"Visualization is powerfully creative. It's like making a movie in your mind."
George Mumford

IMAGINE you're preparing for a crucial game. The ability to visualize or mentally rehearse scenarios—running through plays, strategizing movements, and envisaging success—can be the difference between victory and disappointment. Many components contribute to sporting success, including the ability to see the outcome you desire. Mental rehearsal is a powerful form of cognitive practice that strengthens neural pathways, increases muscle memory, and refines skill execution.

Mental rehearsal taps into the power of imagination and cognitive processes to simulate real experiences. Mental rehearsal will allow you to vividly recreate scenarios, seeing, feeling, and even hearing the surroundings in your mind's eye. This mental simulation reinforces the brain's familiarity with performing tasks, improving confidence and readiness when those situations arise in the future.

HOW DOES MENTAL REHEARSAL WORK?

Mental rehearsal engages the brain in simulating actions or skills without physically executing them. The effectiveness of this technique lies in its impact on the brain's neural processes and physical responses.

When you vividly visualize yourself performing an action, your brain uses the same neural pathways and muscles as it does in physical movement. This neuromuscular facilitation occurs due to the brain's inability to distinguish between real and imagined experiences. Studies employing electromyography (EMG) have shown increased activity in specific muscles during mental rehearsal, signifying neural activation akin to physical execution. When you imagine an action, you are programming your body for when you perform the action. This is why correctly rehearsing the action you want to perform is so important! Thinking about a mistake, like the water hazards on a golf course, increases the likelihood that's exactly what you'll do—splash!

Moreover, mental rehearsal influences the brain's ability to reorganize and create new neural connections (referred to as neuroplasticity). Repeated rehearsal strengthens the neural circuits associated with a particular skill, training the brain to perform better. This process enhances the brain's efficiency in coordinating movements and actions, improving physical execution when the actual activity is performed. Your body becomes "smarter" by adding thinking about correct movement to the task of practicing the correct movement.

A further benefit of visualization techniques is the lowering of anxiety and stress by regulating the autonomic nervous system. Imagining successful performances helps lower cortisol levels (the stress hormone) and decreases activation of the amygdala, the brain's fear center, resulting in a calmer physiological state conducive to improved performance. Therefore, when you spend time thinking about the outcome you want, there is less time to think about mistakes or other elements that will worry you.

An athlete's confidence and self-efficacy is further improved through mental rehearsal. In Chapter 5, the importance of self-efficacy was discussed. Mental rehearsal is a powerful tool to build your understanding of your capabilities. As athletes repeatedly visualize successful performances, they develop a stronger belief in their abilities, translating into improved confidence when facing real competition.

Furthermore, mental rehearsal facilitates learning and skill acquisition. Combining physical practice with mental imagery expedites the learning process. By visualizing and familiarizing themselves with motor patterns, athletes can refine their execution and optimize their performance in their respective sports.

HOW DOES MENTAL REHEARSAL ASSIST ATHLETIC PERFORMANCE?

Mental rehearsal significantly benefits athletic performance. It aids in honing techniques, refining skills, and enhancing overall performance by establishing mental blueprints for success. Athletes who consistently practice mental rehearsal often report heightened confidence, improved focus, and better emotional regulation during high-pressure situations.

Despite its efficacy, there can be barriers to mental rehearsal. One obstacle is the need for more detailed and vivid mental images. Some athletes may find it challenging to conjure clear mental pictures or sensations. Also, distractions or difficulty maintaining focus during mental rehearsal sessions can hinder effectiveness.

Why invest time in learning mental rehearsal? Simply put, it's an invaluable tool for achieving peak performance. Mental rehearsal, when practiced diligently, offers a competitive edge. It allows athletes to cultivate resilience, hone skills, and prepare mentally without the physical toll of constant practice. It empowers athletes to enhance performance, minimize anxiety, and effectively navigate challenging circumstances.

The role of the inner coach is pivotal in mental rehearsal. Think of the inner coach as your guiding voice, directing and refining your mental rehearsal sessions. This self-talk motivates, provides feedback, and helps maintain focus during visualization. Engaging the inner coach can assist in setting clear goals, maintaining concentration, fostering a positive mindset, and optimizing the efficacy of mental rehearsal.

So, how can you leverage mental imagery to activate your neuromuscular system and enhance your physical performance?

Follow these steps:

Step 1: Preparation

Find a quiet and comfortable space, sitting or lying down. Preparation involves seeking a conducive environment that is quiet and free from distractions. This step is pivotal as it allows for undivided attention to the forthcoming mental rehearsal, establishing a mental setup and signaling readiness for focused visualization.

Step 2: Relaxation

Close your eyes and take deep breaths to clear your mind and be present. Relaxation plays a crucial role by helping achieve a relaxed mental and physical state. Deep breathing and relaxation techniques aid in clearing the mind of stress, reducing muscle tension, and heightening focus on the present moment.

Step 3: Mental imagery

Mental imagery involves creating a vivid mental picture of yourself performing a specific athletic activity. Follow these steps to maximize the effectiveness of your visualisation.

Visualization setup: Find a quiet, comfortable space—close your eyes.

Scenario creation: Envision yourself in the exact scenario you wish to rehearse. Imagine the surroundings, from the field or court to the weather conditions and crowd noise. Be as detailed as possible.

Real-time experience: Visualize the movement or action step-by-step as if you were physically performing it. See yourself executing the skill flawlessly, focusing on each movement with precision.

Emotional engagement: Attach positive emotions to your visualization. Imagine the feelings of confidence, success, and accomplishment as you execute the skill perfectly.

Step 4: Engaging muscles

Concentrate on the specific muscle groups involved in the athletic action. Here's how:

Muscle awareness: In the visualization process, focus on the muscles needed for the movement or action.

Muscle engagement: Mentally engage these muscles as if acting. Focus on the sensations of tension, relaxation, and coordination within those muscle groups.

Mind-muscle connection: As you visualize, create a strong connection between your mind and the muscles involved. This helps reinforce neuromuscular pathways and improves muscle execution during physical performance.

Step 5: Sensory engagement

Engage all your senses during mental rehearsal to create a more immersive experience:

Multi-sensory visualization: Alongside visualizing the scenario and engaging muscles, bring in other sensory details. Hear the sounds of the activity—the crowd cheering, the sound of equipment, or nature. Feel the texture, temperature, and pressure related to your activity. Smell the scents present in that environment.

Physical sensations: Imagine the physical sensations you would experience while performing the activity—the wind on your face, the impact of the ball, or the ground beneath your feet. This sensory engagement creates a more comprehensive and realistic mental representation of the performance.

Practicing mental imagery with muscle engagement and sensory involvement enhances the effectiveness of mental rehearsal, improving performance and skill execution when it comes to actual physical practice or competition.

Step 6: Repetition

Practice mental imagery, focusing on muscle engagement and sensory details with each repetition.

WYSIWYG

Sarah, a dedicated track athlete, was preparing for a crucial upcoming race, seeking a breakthrough after several competitions where she struggled to maintain her speed in the final stretch. Determined to enhance her performance, she was eager to fine-tune her mindset for success.

Sarah's coach introduced her to *WYSIWYG*, an acronym for "What You See Is What You Get." This principle encourages individuals to focus on visualizing the desired outcome rather than fixating on what they want to avoid.

Embracing this idea, Sarah made a significant shift in her mental approach. Instead of dwelling on thoughts like "Don't slow down at the end" or "Avoid feeling fatigued," she redirected her focus toward positive and actionable imagery. During her mental preparation sessions, she vividly pictured herself sprinting smoothly and powerfully throughout the race. She visualized her form, imagined the sensation of her muscles working efficiently, and heard the energizing cheers of the crowd as she confidently crossed the finish line.

As Sarah adopted the WSIWYG principle, she noticed a significant change in her mental energy. Shifting away from fixating on potential pitfalls, she channeled her thoughts into visualizing the success she aimed to achieve. This shift in mindset not only bolstered her confidence but also aligned her actions with her performance goals.

On the day of the race, Sarah put her mental strategies into practice. When fatigue began to set in during the final lap, instead of succumbing to negative thoughts, she summoned the mental imagery she had diligently rehearsed. She focused on maintaining her pace, feeling strong, and visualized herself crossing the finish line triumphantly.

Sarah's application of the WYSIWYG principle showcased the valuable impact of focusing on desired outcomes rather than potential setbacks. By concentrating on the positive and visualizing her success, she equipped herself mentally to perform at her peak and significantly enhanced her race performance. This principle eventually evolved into a deeper understanding of (my favorite acronym) WYSIWYSIWYG—"What You Say Is What You See Is What You Get," emphasizing the direct correlation between thoughts, visualization, and actual performance outcomes.

The principle of WYSIWYSIWYG, represents a more advanced and nuanced approach to the initial concept of WYSIWYG. It's also fun to say out loud, go on—try it! It underscores the important relationship between an athlete's thoughts, words, mental imagery, and their actual performance outcomes.

Essentially, "What You Say" pertains to an athlete's inner coach dialogue. This self-talk will influence your beliefs, perceptions, and overall mindset. Make sure your inner coach is guiding you well. When athletes consistently reinforce positive, empowering, and goal-oriented language in their thoughts and verbal expressions, it impacts their mental state and, consequently, their actions.

The phrase "What You See" signifies the mental imagery and visualization an athlete employs. Visualizing success in detail, imagining the desired outcome, and experiencing it mentally contribute to creating a blueprint for future performance. This mental rehearsal helps fine-tune muscle memory, build confidence, and enhance focus and concentration.

Lastly, "What You Get" refers to the tangible outcomes that result from the athlete's thoughts, verbalizations, and mental imagery. When an athlete consistently practices positive self-talk, vividly visualizes success, and aligns their actions with their goals, it strongly influences their performance. The mental state cultivated through these practices often translates into improved focus, determination, and execution during competitions.

As an athlete, adopting the principle of WYSIWYSIWYG, can be a game-changer. Consider your thoughts and self-talk as the first step—what you tell yourself shapes your beliefs, images and actions. By consistently reinforcing positive, motivating thoughts and phrases, you lay the foundation for a confident mindset. Secondly, visualize success vividly. Picture your best performance, feel the sensations, and see yourself achieving your goals in detail. This mental rehearsal primes your mind and body for success. Finally, understand that what you say and visualize translates into outcomes. You're better equipped to perform at your peak when you align your thoughts, words, and mental imagery with your athletic ambitions. Remember, what you say to yourself and visualize can significantly influence what you achieve in your sport.

VISUAL VICTORY: BETTER PERFORMANCE THROUGH VISUALIZATION

Applying mental rehearsal (or visualization) to your sporting journey is limited only to your imagination! Here I will share with you instances where athletes successfully employed mental rehearsal techniques and their particular focus.

Mental rehearsal for *skill improvement* involves vividly visualizing and mentally practicing specific techniques or movements an athlete aims to execute well. In Chapter 2 I introduced you to basketball player, Emily. At one point later in the season Emily was struggling with her free throws. Despite regular practice, she felt inconsistent in her shots during crucial game moments. Mental rehearsal can assist by providing a focused mental space to improve her technique.

For Emily to apply mental rehearsal in improving her free throws, she would benefit from finding somewhere quiet, closing her eyes, and mentally visualizing herself successfully executing the free throw. She should initially concentrate on every detail, from her stance to the ball's release and the follow-through. When mentally visualizing herself successfully executing the free throw, Emily turns her focus to the following elements:

Stance and preparation: This includes positioning her feet, bending her knees, and holding the ball correctly. She can reinforce positive self-talk by saying, "My stance is stable and balanced."

Shot execution: Visualizing the motion of the shot is critical. Emily should mentally go through the complete shooting sequence, including the ball's trajectory, the arc, and the release. She might say, "Smooth release, nice arc, and spin."

Follow-through: Emphasizing the follow-through is the final component. Emily can imagine her arm extending upward after releasing the ball, ensuring that her wrist follows through naturally. She might affirm, "Strong follow-through, wrist straight."

Using specific phrases like these during her mental rehearsal, Emily visualizes and verbalizes the key elements of her technique. This combination reinforces the mental image of a successful free throw while engaging her mind and body in the correct movements. These phrases can aid in creating a more vivid and constructive mental rehearsal, assisting her in translating these mental repetitions into improved performance on the court. By incorporating mental rehearsals focused on refining specific skills into her routine, Emily can enhance her muscle memory, improve her shooting technique, and increase her chances of success during games.

It's important to note that not every athlete wants to continually think of the movements in such small detail, however it is a helpful place to start. Once she has the correct technique in her sights, she may choose to reduce the description to a few key words: "Balance, arc, follow."

As a dedicated soccer player, Mark is known for his accuracy and finesse in taking penalty shots. Mark has been a key player for his team, but lately, he's been struggling with feeling increased pressure during penalty shots, which has affected his accuracy and therefore his confidence.

To utilize mental rehearsal in handling pressure moments, Mark could create a mental scenario of himself confidently stepping up to take a penalty shot. When he visualizes the scene, he can focus on his breathing to stay calm and composed. By picturing the placement of the ball, seeing its trajectory into the goal, and feeling the muscle memory of his foot striking the ball with precision his inner coach is helping him get closer to success.

High-pressure moments are common in sport—it's what makes it so exciting! Here are the steps you can work on to apply mental rehearsal to the crucial moments in your sport:

Create a vivid mental image: Visualize yourself under pressure, focusing on every detail from your approach to the shot.

Controlled breathing: Incorporate controlled breathing techniques to maintain composure.

Positive self-talk: Use affirming and encouraging phrases such as "I am focused and confident" or "I've practiced this countless times, and I can do it."

Feel the scenario: Engage your senses; feel the ball's texture, hear the crowd's noise, and imagine the successful shot going exactly where you want it to.

By mentally rehearsing these pressure moments and visualizing success, you can better prepare yourself for the pressure cooker moments you might face during competition.

Mia is a competitive skateboarder who recently suffered a knee injury during a competition. Mia feels frustrated as she navigates her recovery journey, worried about how this setback might affect her future performance. To utilize mental rehearsal in *injury recovery*, Mia could visualize herself going through each step of the rehabilitation process. She can imagine herself in the gym, doing the exercises designed for her by her trainer. Mia uses her senses to vividly see (and feel) herself regaining strength and flexibility. As she does this, she imagines the muscles engaging and gradually improving her movements.

Whilst no one wants to be injured, it is a common path for many athletes. In the event that you have an injury, here are the steps that can help for undergoing injury recovery.

Visualize the healing process: Imagine yourself undergoing rehabilitation exercises tailored to your injury. Focus on the body's sensations: Feel the muscles engaging and the gradual improvement in movement.

Positive reinforcement: Use positive affirmations like "My body is healing" or "I am getting stronger every day."

Envision successful return: Picture yourself back in action, performing at your peak level.

By employing mental rehearsal techniques, athletes like Mia can facilitate their recovery process, helping them maintain a positive mindset and visualize a successful return to their sport after injury.

Baseball player, Cameron aims to enhance his strategic thinking on the field. As a pitcher, he wants to anticipate the opponent's moves and improve his decision-making during crucial moments in the game. To employ mental rehearsal for *strategy* in baseball, Cameron thinks through various game scenarios. He mentally places himself on the mound, imagining different game situations, like facing a full count with bases loaded or pitching to a strong batter. Cameron visualizes his pitch selection, the batter's likely reactions, and the fielders' positions for each scenario.

By implementing mental rehearsal techniques, baseball players like Cameron can enhance their ability to anticipate game situations, make better-informed decisions, and be more adaptable on the field, contributing to improved performance during crucial game moments.

Journal prompt

What are the strategies in your sport that would benefit from mental rehearsal? Whilst you may not have a plan for every eventuality, using your inner coach to develop a range of situations will help your mental flexibility when new situations arise. You will be used to thinking quickly through different possibilities. To improve your sport IQ and ability to strategize, you can follow these steps:

Visualize game scenarios: Imagine specific competition situations relevant to your role (e.g., in baseball: pitcher, batter, fielder) and visualize your actions.

Anticipate opponents' moves: Consider potential strategies your opponents might employ and plan your countermoves.

Focus on decision-making: Envision making confident and strategic decisions in critical moments. What are the types of decisions you need to make? See yourself doing those well.

Practice adaptability: Visualize yourself adjusting strategies based on different scenarios unfolding in the game.

Aisha is an enthusiastic mountain biker experiencing a performance slump. Recently, her riding has been affected by a lack of confidence, leading to errors and falls on the track.

To break free from this cycle, Aisha visualises success during her rides. She sees herself conquering challenging trails, navigating sharp turns with precision, and accelerating down steep descents with confidence. Aisha visualizes every detail, from maintaining balance to anticipating obstacles, envisioning herself as a skilled and agile rider, dominating the course with determination and skill.

For mountain bike riders aiming to overcome *overthinking errors* through mental rehearsal:

Visualize success: Mentally rehearse ideal race scenarios where you ride at your peak, emphasizing skilled techniques and confident body positioning.

Rebuild confidence: Envision feeling confident and composed during the ride, visualizing successful turns and positive outcomes.

Focus on strengths: Concentrate on your strengths and previous successful races to reinforce a positive mindset.

Regular mental rehearsal: Engage consistently in mental imagery sessions to build resilience and confidence.

By regularly practicing mental rehearsal in mountain bike riding, athletes like Aisha can break free from negatively overthinking, rebuild their confidence, and visualize successful technique. By doing this she will build a more positive mindset, which will result in improved performance on the track.

IN A NUTSHELL

Mental rehearsal in sports is akin to creating a mental playbook for success. It involves vividly visualizing and simulating various game scenarios or movements without physical execution, using the power of imagination to strengthen neural pathways, enhance muscle memory, and refine skill execution. Through this process, athletes can cultivate a more resilient mindset, improve confidence, and better prepare for high-stress situations.

The essence of mental rehearsal involves engaging the brain's neural processes and physiological responses through visualization. By visualizing themselves performing a specific action, athletes activate the same neural pathways and muscles involved in physical execution. Often indistinguishable from real experiences, this process is crucial for enhancing performance.

The role of an inner coach is pivotal in mental rehearsal. This internal guiding voice directs and refines mental rehearsal sessions. Self-talk is crucial in this process, as it motivates, provides feedback, maintains focus during visualization, and encourages a positive mindset. It also helps in setting clear goals and maintaining concentration during visualization.

Journal prompt

Journaling serves as an effective companion to mental rehearsal. It allows athletes to document their mental rehearsal sessions, track progress, and reflect on their experiences. Through your journaling you can record your visualizations, self-talk patterns, and emotional responses, providing valuable insights into your mental states and aiding in adjustments for improved performance.

Journaling the visualization part of your sporting preparation can be a useful communication tool with your coach. You may choose to share the cue words and phrases you use to increase the understanding by your coach of your focus.

Mental rehearsal is more than simply daydreaming; it's a strategic and helpful thinking tool. It's an avenue to bridge the gap between practice and performance, offering athletes a powerful way to prepare their minds for success on the field. By mastering mental rehearsal techniques, engaging the inner coach, and leveraging journaling to track progress and insights, you can improve the consistency and control of your mental performance.

DON'T TELL PEOPLE YOUR PLANS SHOW THEM YOUR RESULTS.

CHAPTER ELEVEN
RISE STRONGER IN TIMES OF INJURY

"Success is not final, failure is not fatal: It is the courage to continue that counts."
Winston Churchill

WHEN INJURIES STRIKE, they're more than just physical setbacks. The psychological impact can be profound in a competitive arena like rugby league. Meet Rachel, a rugby league player sidelined due to a severe ankle injury. Her world turned upside down when she got hurt, leaving her with a feeling of being overwhelmed.

Just following the injury, Rachel said, "Rugby league has been such a huge part of my life. I feel like I've lost a big piece of who I am. It's tough knowing that I can't be out there with my team. They've always needed me, and being sidelined makes me feel helpless. Rugby has always been my escape, my way to unwind from life's pressures—how do I deal without it now? My teammates mean more to me than just teammates; they're my family. I can feel my confidence dropping, and my dreams are slipping away."

Athletes invest so much of themselves into their sport. When Rachel lamented, "Rugby league has been such a huge part of my life. I feel like I've lost a big piece of who I am," she echoed a sentiment familiar to many athletes. The sport becomes woven into their identity, shaping how they see themselves and how others perceive them. A significant injury can shatter this perception, prompting athletes to question their sense of self and purpose beyond the sport.

Rachel's distress about letting her team down—"They've always needed me, and being sidelined makes me feel helpless"—reveals the strong sense of responsibility athletes feel towards their teammates. The bond forged within a team extends beyond the field, creating a camaraderie that fosters a collective reliance. The injury disrupts personal aspirations and triggers guilt and worry about their impact on the team's success.

For many athletes, sports serve as a sanctuary for emotional release. Rachel's concern—"Rugby has always been my escape, my way to unwind from life's pressures—how do I deal without it now?"—highlights the emotional void an injury creates. The absence of physical activity can leave athletes without their primary coping mechanism, leading to heightened emotional distress and uncertainty about managing stress effectively.

Athletes often find a second family among their teammates. Rachel's sentiment—"My teammates mean more to me than just teammates; they're my family"—touches upon the isolation an injury can cause. Not being part of the team activities or sharing the camaraderie of training sessions can create a sense of loneliness and feeling detached.

The dreams and aspirations athletes nurture can feel dashed with a severe injury. Rachel's anguish—". . . my dreams are slipping away"—illuminates the shattered aspirations and uncertainties about the future. The setback of an injury casts doubts on an athlete's ability to fulfill their long-held ambitions.

Lastly, the injury's impact on confidence is important. Rachel's lament—"I can feel my confidence dropping"—hints at the erosion of self-belief that often accompanies injuries. The inability to train or perform at the usual standard can dent an athlete's confidence, raising doubts about their capabilities and creating a fear of being unable to reclaim their former abilities.

Rachel's words really hit home, capturing the true emotional impact of a major injury on an athlete's mind. They touch on some real tough spots—feeling like you're losing a part of yourself, letting your team down, dealing with the emotional fallout, feeling isolated, seeing your dreams take a hit, and struggling with your confidence. It's a real roller coaster of emotions when you're sidelined.

The emotional toll is daunting. Yet, how athletes approach recovery is pivotal, and it's more than just physical rehabilitation. Drawing from extensive experience working with competitive athletes, let's delve into the crucial role of mindset during recovery.

My PhD research focused on elite rugby league players. We tracked their injuries, recovery time, and mental outlook—whether they tended to be optimistic or pessimistic. Initially, we anticipated forwards, prone to more physical confrontations, to have longer recovery periods than backs. But it wasn't that simple.

When we introduced the variable of mindset—how these athletes perceived and interpreted their situations—it became evident that an optimistic outlook significantly impacted recovery. One player, an optimist despite his injury, displayed remarkable resilience. His recovery period was notably shorter than expected for a severe knee injury, outshining his fellow backs.

DEFYING DOUBT: TRIUMPHING THROUGH OPTIMISM

Optimism and pessimism are not just fleeting emotions; they represent habitual thinking that profoundly shapes an individual's understanding of the world. Optimists see the possibilities even in challenging situations. They naturally gravitate towards anticipating positive outcomes and focusing on potential solutions. Optimistic individuals view setbacks as temporary hurdles and approach problems with a mindset of finding constructive resolutions. They maintain a positive outlook, often believing that difficulties present opportunities for growth and learning.

On the contrary, pessimists lean towards expecting the worst in any given circumstance. Their thoughts tend to dwell on setbacks and negative aspects rather than seeking solutions. Pessimistic individuals often find fault in external situations and themselves, reinforcing a cycle of negativity. They may struggle to see beyond the immediate adversity, perceiving it as a definitive and insurmountable barrier.

The following illustrates how two different mindsets might respond to the same situation.

Situation: The athlete has a torn bicep.
Optimist self-talk: "I need to do all my rehab, the better I work at that and get it done, the sooner I'll get back to playing."
Optimist emotions: Determined and motivated.
Optimist behavior: Is compliant with the rehabilitation program. Does exercises as required. Returns to training with the team in 3 months.

Situation: The athlete has a torn bicep.
Pessimist self-talk: "This sucks. I don't think this will ever heal. It doesn't matter what I do. This is the worst."
Pessimist emotions: Frustrated and hopeless.
Pessimist behavior: Partially compliant with rehabilitation recovers slower than expected. Rejoins the team after 6 months and within 10 days reinjures himself.

The response to the identical torn bicep injury in the scenario above shows two markedly distinct outcomes, depending on the event's interpretation. The interpretation is created by our inner coach. The experience during injury is an important example of how the commentary of the inner coach shapes our views, and impacts our behavior and outcomes.

How we react to life's challenges matters significantly. The words we speak aloud (and in our minds), and our reactions during challenging situations heavily influence how individuals understand and handle similar events. The inner coach, in essence, plays a pivotal role in shaping our responses to life's hurdles.

Understanding the impact of these habits of thinking is crucial, especially when facing adversity. The way individuals interpret and respond to challenging situations is less about the event (beyond their control), and more about how they perceive and process it (within their control). Optimism and pessimism become lenses through which individuals view the world, influencing their reactions to setbacks and determining their resilience in the face of adversity. Developing an optimistic mindset, even amidst difficulties, can significantly impact an individual's ability to navigate challenges and bounce back from setbacks.

Moreover, as part of our investigation, we delved into the potential psychological factors that might contribute to an increased susceptibility to injuries. Could an individual's mental approach heighten the likelihood of getting injured? What role might the inner coach play? As the analysis unfolded, I found three significant factors that amplified the risk of sustaining an injury.

The initial factor centered on self-esteem, where individuals with lower self-worth were found to have a higher incidence of injury. Lower self-esteem seemed to lead to decreased confidence, impacting an athlete's focus or physical readiness, thereby increasing the probability of injury.

The second factor involved athletes who became overwhelmed by the thinking of their inner coach. Those who excessively analyzed and fixated on a specific scenario to the extent of developing tunnel vision were at an elevated risk of injuries. This intense mental fixation might impair an athlete's ability to react to dynamic and unexpected situations on the field, potentially leading to an increased risk of injuries.

Lastly, an athlete's time in the sport was identified as a further critical factor. Athletes who started playing in rugby league during their later teenage years faced a heightened risk of injury. This susceptibility might be attributed to the comparatively shorter duration of time learning the sport's intricate motor patterns and skills before reaching the elite level. The lessened exposure and practice time could contribute to less developed reflexes or adequate skill development, thereby increasing the risk of injuries at the elite level.

Rachel's case emphasized that a positive mindset—her self-talk, outlook, and emotional resilience—was a game-changer. Optimism accelerated her recovery, outweighing the predictive power of playing position in injury duration.

Recognizing the impact of mindset is crucial for readers immersed in competitive impact sports like rugby league. Developing an optimistic mindset during injury rehabilitation can be a game-changer, expediting recovery and facilitating a more confident return to the field. Embracing a positive outlook amidst challenges becomes a cornerstone for success, ensuring a stronger and more determined comeback.

REBOUNDING STRONGER: NAVIGATING INJURY SETBACKS WITH RESILIENCE

In sports, injuries often disrupt an athlete's path, posing significant challenges to body and mind. Whether it's a sprain, strain, or a more severe injury, the impact resonates deeply, affecting the individual's physical abilities and emotional well-being. This chapter guides navigating the complexities of injury and rehabilitation, drawing upon the experiences of athletes like Rachel and offering comprehensive strategies to overcome adversity and emerge stronger.

Strategies for rehabilitation

You need a solid strategy for this phase to get back to your sport faster and make the most of your recovery. Here's a practical roadmap to guide you through rehab and keep you on track. I've included questions to challenge you for each step. You don't have to respond to every question but choosing a few to consider in your journal might prove beneficial. Remember, staying curious aligns with a winning mindset—when your inner coach approaches an injury with curiosity it keeps you engaged and less critical and helps manage your emotions while sidelined.

Build your support network: Returning to peak performance isn't a solo endeavor. Just as Rachel had a team of health professionals supporting her, gather your network of experts and trusted individuals who can guide and help you throughout your recovery.

Curious questions you could ask:
- Who can support me best during my recovery, understanding my unique challenges as an athlete?
- How can I expand my support system effectively to ensure assistance during this phase?
- What actions can I take to strengthen my existing connections and make them more reliable?

Express empathy and seek understanding: Recognize the impact of your injury, both emotionally and physically. Be kind to yourself and seek empathy and understanding from those who care about your well-being. Their support can make a significant difference during this challenging time.

Curious questions you could ask:
- How can I better understand the experiences of teammates or others facing similar setbacks?
- How can I show genuine empathy toward those assisting me in recovery?
- What steps can I take to acknowledge and address my own emotional needs during this phase?

Communicate openly: Don't hesitate to share your thoughts, concerns, and emotions about your injury. Clear, open communication with your healthcare team and loved ones contributes to a healthier mindset and better healing.

Curious questions you could ask:
- What strategies can I use to communicate progress and concerns effectively with my healthcare team?
- How can I best articulate my thoughts and needs to my support team?
- What proactive measures can I take to talk openly with coaches about my recovery?

Take control of decisions: Engage actively in your treatment plan. Participate in decisions within the guidance of healthcare professionals. Taking ownership of your recovery fosters commitment and a more involved healing process.

Curious questions you could ask:
- What decisions can I make to enhance my recovery process?
- How can I actively participate in my rehabilitation decisions?
- What steps can I take to ensure I'm in charge of my recovery journey?

Approach recovery strategically: Treat your recovery like a strategic training plan. Set achievable goals and establish a structured plan with your healthcare providers. This approach ensures steady progress and keeps you focused on your rehabilitation.

Curious questions you could ask:
- How can I strategize my recovery plan to maximize its effectiveness?
- What specific tactics can I employ to ensure a systematic approach to rehabilitation?

- What steps can I take to organize and structure my recovery process?

Stay connected to your passion: Keep engaged with your sport or activity, even if it's in a modified capacity. Finding ways to stay involved fosters motivation and a sense of belonging throughout your recovery journey.

Curious questions you could ask:
- How can I keep my passion for my sport alive during recovery?
- What actions can I take to stay involved in my sport even while recovering?
- What strategies can I use to maintain my enthusiasm and connection to my sport?

Maintain focus: Concentrate on the aspects of your recovery you can control. Setting your sights on achievable milestones aids in maintaining a positive mindset and propels you towards full recovery.

Curious questions you could ask:
- How can I stay focused on my recovery goals amidst distractions?
- What methods can I use to maintain concentration during my rehabilitation?
- What strategies can I employ to maintain my recovery objectives?

Offer yourself continuous support: Be your advocate. Encourage yourself, stay realistic about recovery, and acknowledge your progress. Your resilience and self-motivation are pivotal in your journey back to your sport.

Curious questions you could ask:
- How can I provide myself with ongoing encouragement during my recovery?

- What actions can I take to support my mental and emotional well-being throughout this phase?
- How can I remind myself to stay positive and motivated during setbacks?

Watch for red flags: Watch for persistent negative emotions or behaviors. If you experience denial, intense feelings, withdrawal, or reluctance to follow your treatment plan, seek professional support promptly to ensure a proactive approach to your rehabilitation.

Curious questions you could ask:
- What signs should I look for that might indicate complications or setbacks?
- How can I recognize warning signs that could hinder my recovery progress?
- What steps can I take to monitor my recovery and quickly identify potential problems?

Maintain discipline: Maintaining discipline requires a steadfast commitment to the prescribed routine, exercising discipline in adhering to the daily regimen, and resisting the urge to skip or overlook sessions. It involves dedicated perseverance, embracing setbacks as part of the journey, and unwavering focus on the end goal of full recovery.

Curious questions you could ask:
- How can I ensure consistency and discipline in following my rehabilitation routine?
- What strategies can I use to stay disciplined and committed to my recovery plan?
- How can I maintain the same dedication to my recovery as I do to my sport?

Injuries are not just physical setbacks; they test an athlete's resilience, mental strength, and dedication to their craft. Rachel's story and the outlined strategies serve as guiding principles, offering a roadmap for those enduring the athlete's rehabilitation journey. By building a robust support system, staying engaged, and maintaining focus, individuals can navigate the challenges of recovery with determination, fostering a triumphant return to their peak performance.

RETURNING FROM INJURY

Returning to your sport following an injury entails dealing with multiple physical and psychological challenges. One of the foremost hurdles often encountered is the mingling of anticipation and apprehension that comes with the return to training and playing. These conflicting emotions can create doubts about your capabilities and re-injury potential. To navigate this, initiating an open and honest conversation about your concerns is vital. Engaging in conversations with a trusted sports physician or therapist can offer valuable understanding and guidance, building a sense of reassurance and trust in your recovery trajectory. Belief in your body's strength and repair, reinforced by expert advice, is crucial when on this path.

Moreover, the persistence of repetitive negative images related to the initial injury can impede progress. The inner coach plays a pivotal role here; by harnessing the power of mental imagery and visualization techniques, you can reshape these negative images into positive ones. Envisioning successful athletic moves builds a mental environment steeped in belief and confidence. Visualizing strength and recovery builds belief in your capabilities and sets up a mindset conducive to a successful return.

Considerations about the fear of re-injury often linger, affecting full engagement in the rehabilitation process. The inner coach can assist in reframing these fears by using a positive mindset. Addressing these concerns through conversations with healthcare professionals—

expressing worries about potential re-injury or the stability of the affected area—opens avenues for guidance and reassurance. Embracing this vulnerability and seeking expert advice instills a sense of belief and control over your rehabilitation journey. When your inner coach feels more in control, you will feel more confident and your rehabilitation progress will be more predictable.

In essence, successfully returning from injury necessitates collaboration between your inner coach and external expertise. By acknowledging and addressing concerns, reprogramming mental imagery, and seeking advice where necessary, you empower yourself to reclaim confidence, belief, and readiness for a triumphant return to your sport.

Journal prompt

Use your journal to delve deeper into your past experiences with injury. Reflect on what strategies have been beneficial for you in effectively managing these challenges in the past. If you are presently dealing with an injury, consider which aspects of the previous chapter would be advantageous for you to focus on. Spend some time contemplating how you can apply these insights to your current situation.

Sports injuries are more than physical setbacks; they pose complex challenges that extend into an athlete's emotional and psychological realm. Athletes like Rachel grapple with a profound sense of being overwhelmed and disconnected when sidelined due to injury. Her thoughts, shared earlier reveal the multitude of emotions in relation to identity disruption, team responsibility, emotional coping, isolation, shattered aspirations, and confidence erosion. To overcome these challenges, athletes need a well-rounded approach to rehabilitation and return to training and play. By blending inner resilience with expert guidance and employing strategies like building support networks, fostering empathy, communicating openly, and staying focused, athletes can navigate the rehabilitation journey with determination and emerge stronger.

CHAPTER TWELVE
COMPETE WITH BELIEF: THE NEXT LEVEL AWAITS

"Believe in yourself and all that you are. Know that there is something inside you that is greater than any obstacle."
Serena Williams

WELL, that's been quite a journey! Let's recap where we've come to together.

THE INNER COACH AND YOU

Let's zoom in on a critical aspect of your athletic journey—a moment where your thoughts carry tremendous weight. You're standing at the crossroads: will you unwittingly become your toughest opponent, or will you consciously stand tall as your own greatest supporter? Despite the noise from external critics and doubters, there's a powerful voice within: your inner coach. This internal critic can flood your mind with negative, self-limiting thoughts like unwelcome guests overstaying their welcome in your mental space.

Picture your mind as a prized arena, limited yet precious. Every thought, whether empowering or self-defeating, competes for a place in this valuable space. The unhelpful thoughts, impede your progress and stifle your potential. Your inner coach is always in control. Pay attention to what you say to yourself to give yourself the best chance of victory.

Becoming your staunchest advocate is a game-changer. If you can't fully believe in your skills and resilience, how can you expect the world to rally behind you? Sometimes, the path to victory requires allowing your inner coach to lead—guiding you toward your athletic peak through helpful self-talk and guidance.

Freeing your mind from negativity and self-doubt paves the way for a mental fortress built for success, perseverance, and unshakable confidence. Embrace the idea of being your own champion, cultivating a mindset deeply rooted in honesty and helpful self-talk.

Your inner coach is your ally, mentor, and guide. Equip it with strategies to counter negativity: engage in positive self-talk, challenge self-limiting beliefs, and visualize success. Practice gratitude, mindfulness, and self-reflection to nurture your inner coach into a powerhouse of confidence.

Remember, this journey isn't about eliminating challenges but transforming your relationship with them. Embrace setbacks as learning opportunities. Empower your inner coach to guide you through adversities, making them stepping stones toward growth.

As you harness the potential of your inner coach, watch how it transforms your athletic journey. It's not merely about winning trophies; it's about unlocking your true potential and becoming a beacon of inspiration for yourself and those around you. Trust your inner coach—it's the steadfast ally guiding you toward greatness.

JOURNALING 2.0

Journaling has been a constant companion throughout this journey, a guide nudging you toward self-reflection and personal discovery. Perhaps you've taken pen to paper, recording thoughts, epiphanies, or aspirations. Or the ideas resonated within, sparking contemplation and self-analysis. Either way, the path you choose is yours to navigate.

Consider this a challenge—a crossroads where the decision isn't about the book as an interesting read but about utilizing it as a launchpad for personal improvement. Journaling isn't merely about jotting down past experiences; it's a compass directing your future steps. It beckons you to ask: "What's next?"

Reflective journaling isn't confined to revisiting the past; it's a forward-thinking instrument. Imagine the future version of yourself. Who is that individual? What does this future you, do? How does this version of yourself navigate challenges? Contemplate these aspects; let your journal become a tool to create your future.

Through reflection and consideration, your journal transforms into a roadmap charting your trajectory toward growth and success. Use it not just to dwell on past occurrences but to create the blueprint for the version of you ready to step up.

It's the subtle art of blending reflection with anticipation, creating an energy that propels you forward. Journaling isn't solely about dissecting what has been, but crafting what could be. It's a tool for your past, present and future.

So, as you close this chapter, the book becomes a milestone—a signpost in your journey. What happens next rests in your hands. Will it gather dust on a shelf or serve as the catalyst for change? Embrace journaling as a companion in this quest. Let it be the bridge between reflection and action, paving the way for your blueprint into the best version of yourself.

Let's reaffirm the essential lessons from *Belief*.

PRIME YOUR MIND: ACTIVATING YOUR INNER COACH

Chapter focus: Building unwavering belief is a foundational element for achieving athletic excellence.

Summary: A seasoned athlete, Jack faced a common yet challenging hurdle—self-doubt. His story reflects the universal struggle of many athletes despite possessing exceptional skills and dedication. This chapter lays the groundwork to understand how belief shapes an athlete's performance and the power of one's inner dialogue as the "inner coach."

Key takeaways for the competitive athlete:

1. Belief shapes performance: Self-doubt can hinder even the most skilled athletes, influencing confidence and decisions.
2. Inner dialogue matters: The "inner coach" within significantly impacts an athlete's mindset, guiding strategies, and responses to challenges.
3. Belief is cultivable: Contrary to being fixed, belief is malleable and can be changed and strengthened through specific strategies and psychological tools.

Actions for your inner coach:

1. Self-assessment: Acknowledge and evaluate your inner dialogue's impact on your performance.
2. Practice positivity: Cultivate a positive inner dialogue to foster confidence and resilience.
3. Learn and apply: Implement strategies from the book to strengthen your belief system for improved athletic performance.

BELIEFS AND VALUES: THE HEART OF PERFORMANCE

Chapter focus: Understanding values' impact on athletic performance.

Summary: Emily, a talented basketball player, grapples with inconsistency despite her skills. Her journey reveals the mystery of being "consistently inconsistent." The chapter emphasizes the pivotal role of goal setting in addressing her performance fluctuations. It introduces an alternative perspective of integrating values into goal setting to enhance athletic performance.

Key takeaways for the competitive athlete:

1. Recognize values as guiding beacons shaping decisions and behaviors in sports and life.
2. Authentic alignment of values with beliefs and actions is crucial for consistent performance.
3. Identify values through a deliberate process.
4. Living by your values fosters happiness, motivation, and success-driven actions.
5. Cognitive dissonance arises when actions contradict personal values, impacting well-being and performance.

Actions for your inner coach:

1. Explore your core values and align them with your athletic pursuits.
2. Self-reflection on your values, their alignment with actions, and their impact on overall satisfaction and performance.
3. Set values-based goals as guiding lights in achieving desired results.

SHARPENED CURIOSITY: MASTERING FOCUS IN THE RIGHT MOMENT

Chapter focus: Harnessing time orientation for athletic success.

Summary: Jacinta, coach of the Ace Avengers, guides her volleyball team using mindfulness during critical gameplay. The chapter emphasizes the importance of balancing past reflection, present focus, and future planning for peak athletic performance. Strategies highlight curiosity-driven growth and the transformative power of embracing mistakes as learning opportunities.

Key takeaways for the competitive athlete:

1. Optimal performance involves managing thoughts across past, present, and future.
2. Curiosity fuels growth, and mistakes are stepping stones to improvement.
3. Embracing the present moment enhances sports performance significantly.

Actions for your inner coach:

1. Prompt athletes to anchor their focus on the present during competitions.
2. Encourage athletes to journal examples of past, present, and future thinking.
3. Foster a team culture valuing curiosity and seeing errors as pathways to improvement.

FROM FIXED MINDSET TO FLEXIBLE EXCELLENCE: SHIFTING LIMITS TO TRIUMPHS

Chapter focus: Navigating challenges in sports: Embracing adversity and pursuing excellence.

Summary: The chapter promotes the "fortunately/unfortunately" mindset to manage adversities amid the challenges of a World Cup. It advocates shifting focus from perfection to excellence, utilizing psychological tools for growth-oriented thinking, and encouraging practical strategies for athletes to embrace challenges positively.

Key takeaways for the competitive athlete:

1. Adversity management: Reframe negative situations using "fortunately/unfortunately."
2. Excellence over perfection: Aim for progress and personal best, not an unattainable ideal.
3. Psychological tool usage: Embrace a performance mindset, helpful self-talk, and visualization.

Actions for your inner coach:

1. Practice "Fortunately/Unfortunately" reframing.
2. Shift focus to achievable excellence goals.
3. Implement psychological tools for growth-oriented thinking.

CONQUER DOUBT AND NEGATIVITY: UNLOCK YOUR COMPETITIVE EDGE

Chapter focus: Language's role and mental management in sports.

Summary: The chapter underscores language's power in shaping success, emphasizing clear instructions during pressure. It redefines overthinking as strategic thinking—strategies like helpful self-talk and anchoring aid focus. Celebrating victories shifts focus from negativity. Imposter thinking is addressed, offering support strategies for self-doubt.

Key takeaways for the competitive athlete:

1. Positive language molds mental success imagery.
2. Clarity in instructions is crucial during intense moments.
3. Reframe overthinking as a strategic thought process.

Actions for your inner coach:

1. Embrace positive self-talk for enhanced mental imagery.
2. Deliver precise, clear instructions in pressure situations.
3. Strategically manage excessive mental investment for optimal performance.

BELIEF VS. DISAPPOINTMENT: NAVIGATING THE ROLLER COASTER OF EXPECTATIONS

Chapter focus: Overcoming disappointment on the path to success.

Summary: Sarah, an ambitious track athlete, faced a setback after an injury thwarted her championship qualification. The chapter delves into the emotional journey of coping with disappointment. It highlights the impact of acknowledging and navigating disappointment constructively, emphasizing its role in personal growth and resilience.

Key takeaways for the competitive athlete:

1. Disappointment is a natural part of the athletic journey.
2. Rather than rushing past it, navigating through disappointment fosters growth.
3. Embracing setbacks as learning opportunities fuels personal evolution.

Actions for your inner coach:

1. Accept disappointment as a natural emotion, allowing space for personal improvement.
2. Channel emotional energy constructively to navigate setbacks effectively.
3. Reframe setbacks as stepping stones toward personal and athletic development. Become a better athlete because of the adversity, rather than despite it.

CONQUER MENTAL OBSTACLES: STRATEGIES FOR OVERCOMING NEGATIVE BIAS

Chapter focus: Understanding and overcoming the negativity bias in athletics.

Summary: Ashton, a cross country runner fixated on losses, highlights the detrimental impact of negativity bias. It impedes his progress despite numerous victories. The chapter details its effects on athletes' mindset, resilience, and decision-making. Strategies like mental reframing, mindfulness, and defusion help combat this bias for improved performance.

Key takeaways for the competitive athlete:

1. Negativity bias hampers improvement despite victories.
2. Techniques like mental reframing aid in mindset enhancement.
3. Mindfulness and defusion counteract the bias for better performance.

Actions for your inner coach:

1. Encourage mental reframing after defeats.
2. Implement mindfulness practices in training sessions.
3. Guide athletes in practicing defusion techniques for mental clarity.

TRIUMPH OVER TRIALS: HARNESSING HELPFUL THINKING FOR VICTORY

Chapter focus: Understanding the power of optimism in athletics.

Summary: Optimism, essential for performance, involves personalization, pervasiveness, permanence, and hope. Acknowledging negative thoughts rather than suppressing them aids emotional regulation. Reframing worry as excitement, employing cue words, and using the "flush it" method are effective strategies to manage emotions and enhance performance.

Key takeaways for the competitive athlete:

1. Optimism involves personalization, pervasiveness, permanence, and hope.
2. Acknowledge, rather than suppress, negative thoughts for emotional control.
3. Reframe worry as excitement, use cue words, and employ the "flush it" method for better performance.

Actions for your inner coach:

1. Encouraging you to acknowledge and accept negative thoughts without judgment.
2. Teach reframing techniques to perceive worry as excitement.
3. Guide you using cue words and the "flush it" method to effectively manage emotions.

MOOD MASTERY: USING EMOTIONAL RESILIENCE FOR PEAK PERFORMANCE

Chapter focus: Understanding the impact of emotions on athletic performance.

Summary: In the athletic realm, emotions—Sadness, Joy, Disgust, Anger, Fear—play a pivotal role. Effectively managing these emotional states is crucial, fostering resilience and shaping an athlete's success. Embracing emotions as tools for growth, utilizing the inner coach for guidance, and maintaining an emotional response (rather than reaction) through the highs and lows of sport will help you to sustain focus, contributing to peak performance on the field.

Key takeaways for the competitive athlete:

1. Embrace emotions as tools for growth and performance enhancement.
2. Utilize the inner coach to navigate and harness emotions effectively.
3. Maintain a balance between emotions to sustain focus and excellence.

Actions for your inner coach:

1. Encourage self-reflection on emotional triggers.
2. Cultivate gratitude and mindfulness in routine practices.
3. Seek professional guidance for overwhelming emotions impacting performance.

MIND'S EYE MASTERY: CRAFTING YOUR WINNING PLAYBOOK

Chapter focus: Mental rehearsal for athletic performance enhancement.

Summary: Mental rehearsal, a cognitive practice, utilizes vivid visualization and neural engagement to refine skills, enhance confidence, and prepare athletes for success. Simulating actions strengthens neural pathways, improves muscle memory, and optimizes the brain's coordination efficiency. It aids in managing stress, boosting confidence, and enhancing focus during high-pressure scenarios.

Key takeaways for the competitive athlete:

1. Embrace mental rehearsal for skill enhancement and performance preparation.
2. Visualize success vividly, engaging senses and emotions for optimal rehearsal.
3. Utilize controlled breathing and positive self-talk for mental composure during rehearsals.

Actions for your inner coach:

1. Encourage clear goal setting and concentration during mental rehearsals.
2. Guide athletes in leveraging self-talk and visualization for confidence building.
3. Promote journaling to track progress and refine mental rehearsal techniques.

RISE STRONGER: STRENGTHENING THE MIND FOR INJURY AND RECOVERY

Chapter focus: Navigating the athlete's emotional journey post-injury.

Summary: Injuries transcend physical setbacks, impacting an athlete's identity, team bonds, and aspirations. Rachel's circumstances highlights emotional challenges—identity crisis, team disconnection, and shattered confidence. Key insights emphasize optimism's impact on recovery, factors amplifying injury risk, and strategies for a resilient comeback.

Key takeaways for the competitive athlete:

1. Optimism accelerates recovery post-injury.
2. Lower self-worth and mental fixation amplify injury susceptibility.
3. Strategies for rebuilding resilience and reigniting passion.

Actions for your inner coach:

1. Foster an optimistic outlook amidst setbacks.
2. Address self-worth and avoid mental fixation.
3. Rekindle passion through resilient practices.

WHAT'S NEXT? FROM *BELIEF* TO *COMPETE*

When it came time to write this book, I was torn between two ideas. I knew both would be critical to readers' success and debated which one to write first. I wanted to write a book to help athletes create an unshakeable belief to maximize their performance; I also wanted to write a book about how to manage the ups and downs of competition: a book called *Compete*. I had to decide which to write, and I kept flipping between which one to go first. I had created a chicken-and-egg problem, which would be the most logical book to write first. I didn't know where to start. Does competing build belief, or does belief precede competing?

So, I outsourced the decision to the people who will be reading it, the athletes. One of the sporting clubs I work with has a large squad of athletes across different divisions: national, state, and local competition. In addition, the club has a pool of coaches and professional staff that I work alongside to support the athletes. Over several weeks, I presented everyone I encountered within the organization with a question: "Imagine there are two sports psychology books in front of you; one is called *Belief*, and one is called *Compete*. You can only pick up one; which one is it?" Then, I kept an old-fashioned tally in the back of a notebook. My problem wasn't solved after a month of asking, with the tally being an almost 50/50 split. Then, an athlete I have worked with for over a year returned from representative duties, and I posed the question to him. He instantly answered, "Belief." I was curious as to how he was so certain. He had responded definitively and quickly, so I asked him. He replied, "Because, without belief, you can't compete." Decision made. From that moment, I knew which book must be written first.

When belief is absent, you are left with indecision and uncertainty. With belief, you have confidence and are self-assured to make the brave decision to compete, try, and potentially fail, but understand that it is simply part of the pathway to greatness. The next book in this series is *Compete*. It is tailored to assist athletes who have already established a strong foundation and understanding of their own capabilities, enabling you further to develop your psychological skills within the competitive arena. Engaging in competition means bringing forth not only one's physical abilities but also the confidence developed through your inner coach. Success in competition hinges upon successfully navigating interactions with teammates, opponents, coaches, officials, and others. In *Compete,* we will delve into the importance of collaboration, leadership, discerning when and how to react, and other essential competencies.

> Look out for *Compete* at your preferred book retailer by the conclusion of 2024.

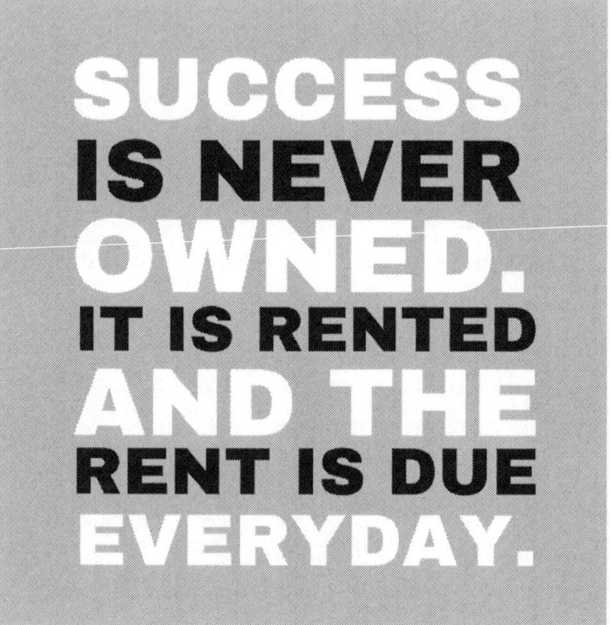

APPENDIX: CREATING CUSTOMIZED VALUES FOR YOUR TEAM

Before identifying values for a team, it is crucial to understand your personal values. Particularly for the leaders within a team, the coaches and senior players need to be clear on their values and discuss those openly to help understand similarities and areas of personal difference. The steps I have outlined earlier in Chapter 2 are the first steps to setting team goals. Know yourself before you start to work on your team.

Walk into the dressing rooms of professional teams, and you will see the values of the team creatively positioned on their walls. Why is it important to place values in such a prominent and visible place, and what role do they have in sporting success? High performers understand that identifying and behaving consistently with values play a role in culture and performance. Making the values visible is a commitment and reminder to the team of the expectations for thinking and behavior at the team's core.

However, I see the most significant danger when values are set and promptly discarded as soon as the season begins. The conversations end, and the values receive little to no engagement as the team gets to business. The setting of values is considered a necessary pre-season task with no connection to the remainder of the season. The teams I have seen be successful at the highest level have always had a very close connection with their values. The values become part of their everyday conversations and offer a lens through which to decide how to act in competition and daily life.

Suppose you google "setting team values." You will find many options for a team. There are many alternative approaches, depending upon the personality of a team or the willingness of a coach and playing group. I don't have only one tried and tested method for team values; I find I need to adapt the methodology on several factors (history of the team together, coaches' views and insights on values, diversity within the team, duration of the season/playing period, individual diversity factors, and time available for the activity). For the benefits of this part of the book, I will offer a method for individual athletes and one for teams. Please know they are not the only options; the methodology must be tailored for the group.

SETTING TEAM VALUES

How, then, do you set values for an entire team? Here is an activity I have done many times, and each time, it has been different but successful. The key to successfully delivering the activity is buy-in from the coaching staff, engagement by the players, and facilitation of the conversation. Where you can, I recommend having someone external to the coaching staff facilitate the discussion to allow the coaching staff to participate fully. There are many ways to finalize values within a team; here, I will share one of my favorite approaches.

<u>Step one</u>: Depending upon the group size, I start by placing the team into groups of four people. There are easy strategies for splitting up a group. For example, with 24 athletes requiring six groups of four, I might point at players and number off, 1-2-3-4-5-6-1-2-3-4-5-6-1-2-3-4-5-6-1-2-3-4-5-6. Now have players sit in groups of matching numbers, so there will be 1-1-1-1, 2-2-2-2 . . . etc. Or you can split the

group after having them stand in order of height or turn it into an icebreaker activity (and a competition) and challenge the groups to form, creating a group with the most differences between its members (e.g., State of origin, favorite colors, birth month).

Why step one is important: I would suggest not letting the team members choose the groups themselves as they will gather with those they know best more often, and the risk of agreement too early and a narrower conversation is likely. The more similar a group, the greater the risk of group thinking. Groupthink occurs when like-minded people get together and too quickly come to a resolution. Keeping the discussions broad and diverse is recommended for this type of discussion.

<u>Step two</u>: With diverse groups selected, I give the groups approximately 20 index cards. I will encourage them to brainstorm a range of values they want to consider for the team. They are to write one value on each card.

Why step two is important: 20 is deliberately chosen as that is a large number of values to consider—realistically far more than anyone would usually select. Therefore, by the time the group reaches values 16, 17, etc., they have probably exhausted most of the critical values the members would like to have considered. It is far better to have more values listed than you need at this stage, as the last few listed will likely not make the final cut.

<u>Step three</u>: The groups are then challenged to reduce their pile of 20 cards down to a maximum of 6–8.

Why step three is important: As mentioned in step two, 20 values are unmanageable and probably lacking in meaning. The group will find some values easy to disregard, and there may be more debate for others. Debate is great and to be encouraged. Have the group discuss the reasons for inclusion and exclusion, and encourage them to work quickly through the exercise.

Step four: With the narrowed list in front of the group, I like them to spend some time with each value, discussing concrete examples of what behaviors would constitute that value. Those behaviors then get written onto the reverse of the card.

Why step four is important: This part of the exercise is critical. It is too common for teams to select tokenistic values to be placed on a wall and never looked at or discussed again. Step four turns the values into practical behaviors that can be witnessed and encouraged. The group must articulate practical and real examples of the values in action.

Step five: This is typically the most unpopular of the stages! With the narrowed list of 6–8 values, I now require the group to reduce their cards to a maximum of four. I tell them to debate what is included and excluded and be prepared to have a robust conversation in picking their final set. Importantly, during this step, I would like to mention that to put a value to one side is not to dismiss it. Group members often become (understandably) wedded to the values they recommend. However, given that we only want a narrowed list, values that the team will still revere won't make the final list but will be followed.

Why step five is important: This is important for two key reasons. The first is that human memory is such that more than four values become quite challenging for teams to hold within their thinking consistently. Secondly, I want the team members to be able to argue for or against the values. The ability to defend what best describes the team and defines the expected behaviors can be likened to the glue that binds the team. It is a sign of great value. If it's not worth fighting for, it's not worth having.

Step six: Now, with the aid of a large whiteboard, it is time to start sharing. At this step, I select one value, write it on the board, and give examples of what action would constitute that value. Invite other groups with the same value to acknowledge that and define the value.

Observe the similarities and discuss any differences. Then, go to the next group and have them share a value. Keep moving around the room until every value is on the whiteboard.

Why step six is important: I like to allow all groups to contribute to the discussion, so I don't let one group immediately share all four of their values. If a group shares all four of its values, you run the risk that the final group won't have anything left to share!

<u>Step seven</u>: With all the values on the board, it is time to consolidate some ideas. For example, one group may have offered perseverance and another relentlessness. The group may decide that these two values are suitably similar and can be combined. At this stage, I wouldn't choose one value name over the other but instead place them together: perseverance + relentlessness. You may write them together or use another colored whiteboard marker to join them with a line or arrows.

Why step seven is important: Here is where the curiosity of the group and developed thinking can be shared. The group discussions around the values are informative. Listen for discussions where large group endorsement is evident; listen for raised voices or strong emphasis. I once had a team use the value, dominate, and the non-verbal reaction of the team to the word made it abundantly clear that this would be one of our finalized values.

<u>Step eight</u>: The next stage is to finalize the values to the final 3–5 values you will settle upon. This is where you will need to make a call on how best to achieve this aim. You may vote and continue discussions where further argument for/against values exists. Alternatively, you might determine the favorite values (to include) and the least favorite (to exclude) and continue to preen the list. Or you may put all the values back in front of the small groups and have them try to finalize them down to the last few. You may also defer this decision to the leadership group (if you have one) or ask the coaches to weigh in on the discussion. Be aware that if/when the coaches do this, it will

significantly impact decision-making. Therefore, depending on how much "sway" a coach wants on this point in the decision-making, they must choose their words carefully.

Step nine (bonus step): I highly recommend this final step. This is where I work with the team to redraft the value's name to something specifically meaningful to the group. The biggest criticism I have of many of the team values I see is that they could be the values of any team for any sport. Using words that reflect the name/branding of the team can make a big difference in the level of engagement with the values. For example, when I worked with the Papua New Guinea Orchids (National Women's Rugby League Team competing at the Rugby League World Cup), we successfully chose value words specific to PNG culture. One of the values that was chosen was gratitude. I love gratitude as a value, particularly for its element of well-being and its link with high performance. But to be honest, it is a word that is so often used now in sporting circles it has almost lost some of its gravitas. To be clear—I am a massive fan of gratitude, but you don't want teams feeling obligated to use a value because the word is widely known and used. Fortunately for our team, there is a word in Tok Pisin (the native language in PNG) that captures the essence of gratitude with joy. That word is Hamamas—I am confident we were the first (if not the only) team in the world to have Hamamas as a value. I knew we were making progress with our values conversation when, after our first game (and team victory), the players were in the dressing sheds with the coach, and he paused while the group listened closely, and he smiled, nodded, and said "Hamamas". Bringing in the values in celebration moments and disappointment makes all conversations easier.

Timing: I would recommend pacing the group through this activity. I typically get through steps 1–7 in one session (usually 60–90 minutes), but if there is fatigue, it may be worth giving the group time to think through further before finalizing. You will need to make this call, depending on the group. If you are working the group through the activity when they are mentally tired, they will come to a resolution too quickly to finish it.

This methodology is my favorite for working with teams on their values. I like it because the team spends time working through a broad range of values, has lots of input, and can articulate what actions and behaviors are consistent with the values. However, determining your team values must be more than a few words on the team wall. Making the team values a living, breathable part of the discussion, will keep your team clear on the shared expectations of the direction from the lighthouse.

Once your values are established, integrate them into as many activities as possible. If you're doing a team review, put them up as a reminder before you start the discussion. It will assist in setting expectations around the conversation. If you go out to a practice session, mention a value as you begin the brief, "Today's conditioning session will improve our cardiovascular fitness. We're better equipped to keep our 'relentless' mindset on the field when we're fitter."

Encourage other roles within the team, such as the Manager, Physiotherapist, and Assistant Coach (if you have one), to use the values in their discussions. I took the values further for the Rugby League World Cup Campaign 2022. We were there through the chill of an English winter, so I had four beanies made up with a value embroidered on the front of each. Then, depending on the session I was running or the players' training, I would wear the most appropriate beanie. A walking billboard if you like for the team values! For example, I ran a leadership session based on sibling position (which I outline in *Compete*). For that session, I wore the beanie that said Yumi Femili (We are family), an important value for the team. Coincidentally, I am writing this section of the book on a plane heading to Port Moresby, Papua New Guinea, in the middle of summer. I have left the beanies at home!

ABOUT DR. JO

Dr. Jo is often referred to as the psychological Indiana Jones of success! With over twenty-five years in the realm of sports psychology, she's on a quest to uncover the secrets behind peak performance.

She finds joy in running with friends (then drinking coffee with them!), going on adventures with her husband and two sons, and reading and watching whatever sport she can! You can connect with Dr. Jo at www.drjolukins.com

facebook.com/DrJoLukins

x.com/Dr_Jo_Lukins

instagram.com/dr_jo_lukins

A NOTE FROM DR. JO

If you enjoyed *Belief*, I would be grateful if you let others know so they can gain your insights on elite performance. If you leave a review for *Belief* on the site from which you purchased the book, Goodreads or your own socials, I would love to read it!

Email me the link at excel@drjolukins.com.

Hamamas, Dr. Jo

STAY CONNECTED: WITH DR. JO

Elevate your personal and professional game with The Locker Room's positive psychology insights.

Dr. Jo presents an exceptional avenue of connection through The Locker Room, serving her audience on two dynamic platforms: a weekly podcast and an insightful monthly newsletter.

Step into the world of The Locker Room, where Dr. Jo's engaging and competitive spirit takes center stage. With a wealth of professional experience and academic expertise, she delves into well-being, happiness, and success, offering her community a boundless source of inspiration.

Tune into the Locker Room

Whether pursuing the latest research in personal excellence or practical guidance for enhancing your life, her newsletter delivers a wealth of wisdom directly to your inbox.

Sign up for newsletter and receive your free Confidence Checklist

READ MORE WITH DR. JO

The Elite: Think like an athlete, succeed like a champion. Ten things the elite do differently. 2019

In the Grandstands: The sporting parents guide to raising a confident and happy teen in the highs and lows of youth sports. 2020

The Game Plan: Your 5-month coaching program to champion high performance habits (High Performance Thinking). 2022

The Elite and The Game Plan 2 in 1 Book: Champion your success with elite habits to unleash your winning potential with 10 proven strategies and high-performance coaching program. 2023

Belief: Building unshakeable confidence. 2024

In Press:
Compete: Getting the results you deserve.

The Whistleblower: The Mental Toughness Rulebook for Referees and Umpires.

BONUS OFFER: THE GOOD SLEEP GUIDE

So much of your functioning is dependent upon your sleep.

Sleep is a critical part of your day when you can dream, repair your body, rest, and process information. There is no doubt that sleep is our best friend, but it can also be our worst enemy. The quality and quantity of our sleep is where we can improve our fitness, sports performance, decision-making, and mood.

If your mind and body are crying out for more rest, *The Elite Sleep Guide* will help. Download your free copy of *The Elite Sleep Guide* at www.drjolukins.com/the-elite

FACEBOOK GROUP

Join Dr. Jo in a community of like-minded individuals in her Facebook group, Winning Strategies. The group offers practical, winning strategies for the ambitious and curious.

Dr. Jo simplifies complex concepts and guides ambitious individuals to develop mental toughness, increase resilience, and achieve their goals. Through Winning Strategies, members access exclusive resources, support, and training to overcome challenges and reach their potential easily. It's free to join now!

www.facebook.com/groups/winningstrategies

Made in the USA
Columbia, SC
12 September 2024